Contents

G000122933

1. Thinking About Power

Contradictions in Development

Many of the readers of this little book will have been involved in some form of 'development action' here in Britain or as volunteers in the Third World. Probably most of you became active in development because you were aware of the obscene gap in living standards between rich and poor countries and wanted to do something about it, wanted to contribute — albeit in a small way — to Third World development. Now, having become involved, do you feel you have contributed to development, either through volunteering or through activities in Britain? Have you come to a view of what causes development, of how it can best be achieved, and of what your own role can be?

Can your theory of development accommodate the following facts?

Volunteering: idealism frustrated

A volunteer teacher, keen and idealistic, ends up teaching English in an urban, fee-paying secondary school in Cameroun. The fees are so high that only the well-off can send their children there. The curriculum is extremely academic and unrelated to the development needs of the country. Before volunteering, the volunteer taught in a large comprehensive in a poor part of London. She leaves before the end of her two year term, feeling that she could make more of a contribution teaching under-privileged kids in Inner London than the offspring of the Camerounian upper class.

Another volunteer, equally keen and idealistic, ends up teaching more or less everything in a Harambee school in Kenya. He immerses himself in the project, feeling that this is what he came to the Third World for: the school is in a poor rural area, the children are poor and, above all, both children and the community in general really want education. The school is a self-help project, started by the community. But later, the volunteer begins to have doubts. What is the education for? He realises that it's to enable the students to leave the village and to get a salaried job in the city. The education he's providing is for the very few who will succeed in this. It's of no relevance for the majority who fail and who will have to make their lives in the countryside. The curriculum contains nothing that will help them improve rural life. Agriculture is barely mentioned, although 95% of the students will have to make their living from it.

"AND WHAT DID THEY TEACH YOU TODAY SON?"

"AMO, AMAS, AMAT"

"... EDUCATION'S A WONDERFUL THING"

A volunteer secondary school teacher in Malaysia finds herself in a job which could equally well be done by a Malaysian graduate. She wonders why she has been sent to Malaysia merely to contribute to graduate unemployment. Could it be something to do with competition with the Peace Corps? With the desire of the British Council to maintain a British presence in Malaysia?

A volunteer technical instructor in Nigeria feels secure in that he is at least teaching a useful skill: any country needs skilled electricians. But, once again, the school's graduates all go off to the towns in search of jobs. The volunteer wonders how long it will be before anything is done for the people in the rural area where he lives. When will the country's development, centred as it is in the towns, begin to affect them?

5

A volunteer physiotherapist in Bangladesh realises that the large modern hospital where she works absorbs an enormous proportion of the country's health budget, but serves only a tiny minority of the population. The health needs of the rural majority are largely ignored. Wouldn't the health budget be better spent on rural health centres? And should physiotherapy receive any government funds at all? In a country where basic health problems are caused by malnutrition, poor water supplies, lack of immunisation against preventable diseases, shouldn't physiotherapy come very low on the list of priorities?

A volunteer midwife in a small mission hospital in Malawi feels that she is making a contribution to health care in the area, especially through her educational work in the mother and child clinic. But overall she finds the hospital paternalistic. It does not encourage local participation. People are made to feel that health is brought to them by white-coated professionals from the outside. But shouldn't the community be involved in health care? Shouldn't she be training community health workers? Given the scarcity of professionals, isn't this the only way of making health care available to all?

All these volunteers feel that they're in a contradictory situation. Most of the people in their host countries are desperately poor. The volunteers want to help them — but somehow their work never seems to be of direct benefit to the people they really want to help, and may not even be of indirect benefit. What's going wrong? Why are their good intentions frustrated?

Looking further afield, there's much else that's going wrong with the 'development process':

Baby foods: selling the baby killer
You don't have to be a medical expert to see that breast feeding is much safer than bottle feeding in Third World conditions. Firstly, poor people can't afford to buy enough baby milk powder, so the baby often gets over-diluted milk. Secondly, bottle feeding often leads to infection, because most Third World families have no way of sterilising the bottles. A survey in Chile showed that babies bottle fed for the first three months had a mortality rate *three* times as high as breast fed babies.[1] The UN Protein Advisory Group has concluded that baby foods should only be distributed in Third World countries if free of charge and under medical supervision. But, despite the dangers, bottle feeding is spreading rapidly in Third World countries. The big multinational companies that produce baby foods are actively promoting bottle feeding — 'expanding their markets' — through advertising and other forms of sales promotion: giving free samples and free feeding bottles, and employing sales-girls dressed as nurses to give talks on infant nutrition. The companies have said that the Third World is becoming an increasingly important source of profits. When criticised for their unethical sales promotion techniques, Nestles replied that competition forced them to continue: other companies would use these techniques; so, if Nestles refrained, it would lose its markets without the Third World consumer gaining anything.

Brazil: growing with poverty

Brazil is loudly proclaimed to have experienced an economic miracle. Between 1967 and 1973 the gross national product (GNP) grew at over 10% per annum.[2] This high rate of growth was largely made possible by multinational firms, which have invested very heavily in Brazil in recent years.[3] But the economic miracle did not improve living standards. By 1970, it is estimated that 74% of the population had real earnings of *less than* the minimum subsistence level laid down in 1958.[4] And while in 1965 (a year after the military coup) it was necessary to work in Sao Paulo for 87 hours to earn enough money to buy basic food supplies for one month, by 1974 155 hours of work were required.[5] Overall, the rich got richer and the poor got poorer:

Brazil's Economic Miracle and Shares of Income

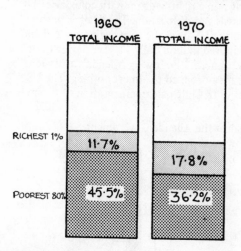

J.C. Duarte, *Aspectos da Distribuicao no Brazil em 1970*, (Piracicaba, ESALQ-USP, 1971).

The effects of the economic miracle are most starkly shown by the infant mortality figures. Between 1940 and 1960, infant mortality in the Sao Paulo region fell by more than half. But between 1962 and 1975, the period of rapid growth, it increased by 45%.[6]

Hunger: land surplus, food shortage

Hundreds of millions of people are starving throughout the world. The UN's Food and Agricultural Organisation says that 460 million would be a 'cautious' estimate of the number of people suffering from malnutrition in the Third World (excluding the Asian Communist countries).[7]

We are told there is not enough food to go round. Food prices rocketed in the early '70s as grain shortages appeared and world stocks fell to dangerously low levels. The UN called a world food conference. But how real was the

7

shortage? Between 1968 and 1970, the major grain producing countries reduced their grain growing area by a third, because of 'overproduction' in the '60s.[8] If the acreage under grain hadn't been reduced, these countries could have produced *90 million* more tons of grain during 1969–72 than they did. In 1973 the UN Food and Agricultural Organisation said that *8 to 12* million tons of grain would help the most famine-hit countries — India, Bangladesh, Pakistan, Tanzania and the Sahel — 'avoid the worst'. This represents less than one percent of the world's grain harvest. Clearly, famine does not arise because the world cannot produce enough food.

Chile: the US interferes
In 1970, Salvador Allende was democratically elected President of Chile, heading a government committed to a socialist transformation of the country. In 1973, his regime was overthrown in a right-wing military coup, after 18 months of increasing economic crisis and dislocation. The Allende government faced intense hostility from the US from the very beginning. Aid and loans had amounted to several hundred million dollars a year during Chile's previous Christian Democrat government.[9] Following Allende's accession, the US government ensured that they dropped to almost nothing. The US refused to help with Chile's debts until Chile paid compensation to the copper

The US Uses the Aid Weapon against the Allende Government

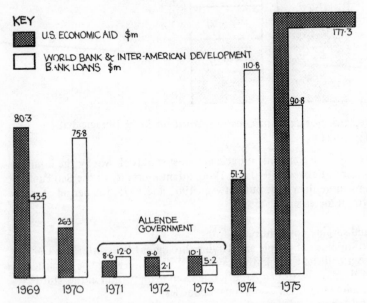

W. Goodfellow, *Chile's Economic Crisis: 1976 and Beyond,* International Policy Report, Vol. II, No. 2, Sept. 1976, Centre for International Policy, Washington DC.

companies, Kennecott and Anaconda, whose mines were nationalised in 1971. Allende refused to pay compensation on the grounds that the companies had been earning excess profits for years. Between 1915 and 1968 they made over $2 billion in profits from their operations in Chile, but reinvested less than one-fifth in the country. Their rates of profit in Chile were many times higher than in their operations in the rest of the world.[10]

"I DON'T SEE WHY WE NEED TO STAND BY AND WATCH A COUNTRY GO COMMUNIST DUE TO THE IRRESPONSIBILITY OF ITS OWN PEOPLE"

(HENRY KISSINGER)

The US did not confine itself to the use of economic weapons. During 1970–73, the CIA spent $8 million in Chile on political destabilisation aimed at overthrowing the Allende regime. This was directly authorised by Nixon and Kissinger. The US had been channelling money to Allende's opponents since 1964 in the hope of preventing Allende from getting elected.[11]

Why does it happen?

Is there any connection between these facts, any pattern lying behind them? Some of them are enough to make you feel that things have gone mad: people are starving, but land is taken out of production and food is thrown away; desperately poor families pay for baby foods which increase the danger that their babies will die; GNP in some Third World countries is growing fast, but most of the people are becoming worse off; people need skills and training, but the education they receive is unrelated to their needs; they desperately need basic health care, but money is concentrated on sophisticated modern medicine. And why drag Chile into this discussion? Isn't what happened in Chile a matter of politics and ideology, not development? I want to argue that these are neither isolated instances of lunacy, nor unrelated to development because 'political': I believe they are results to be expected of an international system dedicated to the pursuit of private profit.

Such a system — or, to call it by its right name, capitalism — tends to concentrate the ownership and/or control of economic resources in the hands of a relatively small elite.[12] Concentration of economic power leads to concentration of political power in the hands of the same group, even in countries which are electoral democracies. Political democracy only goes part of the way towards diffusing power more widely in society. Firstly, it does not deprive the elite of its economic power. Secondly, it does not deprive the elite of its enormous influence on all the organs of government and, more generally, on the ruling ideology of society. Its control of the media and of educational institutions gives the ruling class immense power over people's minds. Most Third World countries are not electoral democracies, so the political power of the national and international economic elite is much more obvious.

Whether the system is formally democratic or not, it operates in the interests of the powerful, which generally means the economic elite – the landowners, mineowners, the managers and owners of capital. The needs of the mass of the people are neglected until they win the power to force the system to take notice. *So, if this theory is correct, eliminating poverty – which is what 'development' is all about – means winning the power to force the system to attend to the needs of the poor majority rather than of the wealthy elite*. This implies that development *must* be a matter of politics, for it means that development is about power – and power is the stuff of politics. It further implies that development must be a matter of struggle, because no ruling group gives up its power without a fight.

Let's consider the examples again. I think they show that development is about power: they show that the 'private profit' system serves the elite, the powerful, and that people are poor because they are powerless. I think the examples also show how the elite perpetuates its control against the opposition of the oppressed. If we agree that development means breaking this control, the examples show what we are up against.

Poor means powerless means poor

Consider the volunteers. They were frustrated because they felt they weren't helping the people who really needed help. The education systems they were working within were all to some extent elitist: either they catered for the children of the existing elite (as in Cameroun), or they prepared a tiny minority of the poor to enter the elite (Kenya). These examples are not untypical of the experience of most volunteers in education. For, in most Third World countries that volunteers serve in, the rural poor haven't yet won the power to force the educational system to respond to their needs.

The medical volunteers found much the same situation. The health system was based on Western, curative medicine. Only rich countries can afford to extend this type of health care to all their citizens. In poor countries, adopting such a system inevitably means neglecting the needs of the masses, while the urban elite is served by expensive, sophisticated hospitals which preempt the lion's share of the health budget.[13]

Population per Medical Doctor
in Urban and Rural Areas, in Selected Countries

Country	Year	*Population/medical doctor*		
		Nationwide	*Urban*	*Rural*
Pakistan	1970	7,400	3,700	24,200
Kenya	1969	12,140	800	50,000
Philippines	1971	3,900	1,500	10,000
Honduras	1968	3,860	1,190	7,140
Colombia	1970	2,160	1,000	6,400
Iran	1967–70	3,752	2,275	10,000
Panama	1969	1,790	930	3,000

Source: World Bank Health Sector Policy Paper, March 1975, Annex 8.

Take the food problem. Why are people hungry? Obviously, not because there isn't enough land in the world, nor because there are too many mouths to feed. People are hungry because they do not control resources: either the land itself, or money to buy the produce of the land owned by someone else. The use of land, the most basic resource of all, is controlled by the elite.

In the Third World land ownership is very highly concentrated. For example, in South America, 17% of the landowners control 90% of the land. In Asia (excluding China), the top 20% of landowners control 60% of the arable land.[14] What does the landowning elite do with the land? Obviously, the landowners (who increasingly include multinational corporations) use it to make profits, and this generally means producing cash crops for export rather than feeding the hungry people of the Third World. Because the hungry are poor, nobody can make a profit by selling to them. If they had political power, they could force their governments to redistribute the land. But, in most Third World countries, the landowners have political as well as economic control.

The baby foods example shows again how the system brings profit to the powerful — in this case, the baby food corporations — at the expense of suffering for millions of Third World families. The system is basically irresponsible: it must therefore be forced to consider the social costs of its activities. Why don't Third World governments control the baby food and other multinationals? Often they're not powerful enough to do this, particularly in those countries where the same multinational food corporations are the major purchasers of their export crops. And in any case, the multinationals make sure that key members of the governing elite are personally profiting from their activities.

In Brazil, the multinationals make profits, and the Brazilian ruling class shares in the spoils — but, as it is all based on the intensive exploitation of Brazilian labour, most Brazilians are excluded from the benefits of faster growth. Effectively, trade unions are outlawed, strikes are illegal.[15] Without

I <u>DO</u> LIKE A NICE
'PICK-ME-UP' THIS
TIME OF DAY...

the right to strike, workers are powerless to resist exploitation. Hence the military regime has been able to attract foreign investment (mainly from the US) with promises of a 'cheap and docile' labour force (i.e. one that is prevented by force from organising). Brazilian workers will only share in the gains from economic growth when they become powerful enough to challenge the power structure.[16]

How does the elite keep control?

A system which ignores the needs of the mass of people inevitably creates opposition. The oppressed people of the Third World are not passive victims. To a greater or lesser extent, and although often faced with overwhelming force, they are struggling against exploitation and repression. The process of economic development itself creates the conditions for an intensification of the struggle. As workers are concentrated in mines, plantations and factories, they gain the chance to organise and so to use the only power they have: the power of numbers.

Ruling groups everywhere rely on two methods to keep control: physical force and 'mind control'.

Physical Force
In Brazil, the use of force has been obvious enough. The country is ruled by a repressive military regime which has destroyed all democratic rights. The US government has backed the Brazilian military's 'forceful' regime with considerable quantities of economic and military aid. This is partly because of the US business elite's very large stake in the Brazilian economy, but more generally because Brazil is seen as following 'the American way' and therefore as a bulwark against communism in Latin America.[17]

In Chile, the international and Chilean business elites began to lose control when Allende came to power. Allende and his supporters attributed continued Chilean poverty — after 150 years of independence — to economic dependence on the US: US firms controlled most of the modern sector of the Chilean

US Control of the Chilean Economy in 1970

Sector	*US-owned Multinationals' Share of Total Production*
Car assembly	100%
Tobacco	100%
Copper fabricating	100%
Radio and TV	nearly 100%
Advertising	90%
Copper production	80%
Industrial & other chemicals	60%
Iron, steel and metal products	60%
Petroleum products and distribution	over 50%
Machinery and equipment	50%
Rubber products	45%

Source: Cockcroft, Frundt and Johnson, 'The Multinational Companies' in Johnson (ed.), *The Chilean Road to Socialism*, (Doubleday, 1973), p. 13.

economy and took most of the gains of economic growth. Allende saw that development had to mean breaking the power of the multinationals, and of the Chileans who had profited from collaborating with them. But the system would not allow Chile to escape. Finally, the Chilean military used force to gain control, actively backed by Chilean business as represented by the Christian Democrats, by US companies and by the US government. Since the coup, the Brazilian 'model' — attempts to attract massive foreign investment on a basis of cheap labour ensured by repression — has also been applied in Chile.

13

Mind Control

'Mind control' is more subtle than physical force and ultimately probably more important. The ruling elite exerts its power over people's minds through a host of institutions: education, politics, religion, advertising, the media. Its aim is to legitimise the existing political and economic system by giving people a set of values which make the system seem 'natural', inevitable and right. To the extent that mind control is effective, it makes physical force unnecessary.

'Mind control' concerns the very 'thinking tools' you give people, the frame of reference within which their process of thought is contained. If you teach people to think with the concepts of heaven and hell, sin and forgiveness, you give them tools for thinking, but you also put limits on their range of thought. If you teach them such terms as 'surplus value', 'alienation', 'paper tigers' — once again you liberate them but yet you chain them.[18]

We can see these forces at work in some of our examples. Take the case of baby foods. Why do poor people voluntarily make their own situation worse? No one forces them to buy baby foods. Physically, it is true, they are not forced. But they are vulnerable to the pressures exerted by the other side — the multinationals. Because of their immense economic resources, the companies can invest heavily in advertising and sales promotion. Bottle feeding is

presented as Western, modern and progressive. In Third World countries where all the people with power are seen to wear Western clothes, drive Western cars, and come from, or are trained in the West; where you learn from an early age in school that to get on you must learn a Western language and forget your own; where everything local has low status, everything Western is prized – in such a society, is it surprising that people buy baby foods?

To return to the volunteers: we have seen that many were serving in more or less elitist educational systems. This means that they were part of the ruling group's 'mind control' in their host countries. Such educational systems not only serve to select those who will become members of the elite, they also instil values – in those who fail as well as those who succeed – which help maintain the whole social structure. This sort of education is based on the goal of individual success, on competition rather than collective effort. This is appropriate to a competitive, 'free enterprise' social system. If people feel that they can through individual effort join the elite, they are less likely to challenge the power structure. And those who fail educationally (the majority) will be more inclined to blame their poverty on their own inadequacy (inability to join the elite) rather than on an unjust social system. Where educational competition is very intense, and only a tiny minority can succeed, as in most Third World countries, this sort of education produces a 'nation of failures' – and at the same time makes the strong stronger.

Even medical volunteers contribute to 'mind control'. Feelings of inadequacy and powerlessness generated by the educational system are likely to be strengthened by a health system in which medical knowledge is the exclusive preserve of very highly trained professionals. If doctors are seen as the only providers of health, ordinary people will feel powerless to do anything themselves about their health care. Also, their dependence on the authority which provides the doctors will be strengthened.

And, of course, volunteers tend to have another 'mind control' effect: they strengthen Western propaganda by personifying the best aspects of the 'Western way of life'.

Won't development bring justice?

Maybe you're thinking – 'All this is very obvious. I know that some countries are more powerful than others – obviously the US is more powerful than Chile. I know that Third World governments are generally corrupt and often repressive. The ruling classes there use their power to exploit their poorer fellow citizens. But the important question to consider is: how is the whole world economic system developing? Won't the process of economic development iron out these disparities of power and wealth? After all, isn't this what happened in the rich countries? As the standard of living has risen, both power and wealth have become more equally distributed. Our history shows that economic progress is accompanied by political progress. As countries become more advanced economically, isn't there a tendency towards democracy? The more advanced the economy, the more educated a work force is required — and it is more difficult to deny educated people their political rights.'

If all this is true, then the solution to the kinds of problems illustrated earlier in this chapter is to help Third World countries follow the road to development taken by the rich countries. This view is something like conventional development economics wisdom. Of course, people realise that the development process took a very long time in the rich countries and they recognise that, because of their appalling poverty, Third World countries don't have that much time. But people who hold these views are optimists. They think that the development process can be speeded up for today's poor countries. Their arguments go something like this: 'We in the West can help do this by sending trained people, and by giving some of our wealth to help them build new industries and modernise their agriculture. The Third World countries will have the advantage of being latecomers. They'll be able to use the scientific and technical discoveries made over a long period in the West.'

'Follow the road to development taken by the rich countries' — what does that mean? How did these countries get so rich? Most people (whatever their political views) would probably agree that the West became rich because of the establishment of capitalism. Unlike previous economic systems, for example feudalism, capitalism has an inbuilt tendency towards growth. Under capitalism, producers are forced to search for new and more efficient production methods. If they don't, their competitors will force them out of business. These incentives to innovation did not exist under feudalism. So, believing that capitalism has enriched the West, and that it brings in its train a fairer and more just political system, many people argue that Third World countries should also try to develop along capitalist lines. They may recognise that the process involves some injustice, but hold that it is the quickest way of achieving a better standard of living for all.

But this conclusion begs some fundamental questions. Is the example of the West relevant? The world is very different now from what it was when the West began the process of capitalist development. The rich countries didn't have to try to develop in a world already dominated by a few very advanced and powerful countries. They didn't have to develop after already being underdeveloped by colonial exploitation. Maybe being a latecomer is not an advantage but a hindrance as far as development is concerned. It's not that easy to compete when you're starting from a position that's so far behind.

Given these factors, is it really going to be possible to speed up the process of capitalist development? Aren't the people who recommend it underestimating its costs? In the rich countries, it took a very long time before the majority of people won their share of the new wealth. In the early stages of the process, the standard of living probably declined for most people — as, for example, when the peasants were forced off the land during the enclosure movement in England in the 16th Century.[19] Or later, when these landless labourers were super-exploited in the factories of the industrial revolution.

Are our economists and planners now clever enough to avoid these miseries? Or will capitalist economic development in the Third World still require a reduction in the standard of living of the mass of people, people already at a barely subsistence level, before they can share in the benefits of economic advance?

What is our role?

In the next few pages, I will be trying to answer some of these questions. But in the meantime, you may be wondering what all this has to do with you. Perhaps you think that it's for the Third World countries themselves to work out their development strategy, and that we should then help them as best we can. I don't think this neutrality is a tenable position because the power holders in our own societies are very much involved in the type of development strategy chosen by the Third World — they are certainly not neutral observers. They may tolerate continued stagnation in some Third World countries, while promoting a form of capitalist development in others. In both cases the Third World remains within the Western economic system and the Western political orbit. But countries that try to break out of their poverty through socialism will find that the Western power structure fights hard to prevent them from following this path. The experience of Chile, described above, is only one example; others are Guatemala, Vietnam, Cuba, the Dominican Republic, Angola.

Because Western governments are involved in the Third World's choice of development strategy — or, to put it more simply, in Third World politics— it also becomes our problem. We can't avoid the issue of whether our governments are doing the 'right thing', whether they are helping or hindering the Third World's attempts at development. And before we can decide this, we have to make up our minds on what is the best road to development. So the questions raised above are vitally important. Our answers will affect our views on 'what we can do as concerned individuals.'

Notes and References

1. See 'Infant Feeding and Infant Mortality in Rural Chile' Plant and Milanesi, *Bulletin of the World Health Organisation*, 1973, 48, 203. Also see UN Protein Advisory Group references quoted in Mike Muller, *The Baby Killer*, second edition, (War on Want).
2. *UN Yearbook of National Accounts Statistics 1976*, Volume 2.
3. For example in 1966, multinational corporations accounted for 64% of total net profits in four of the most dynamic Brazilian industries (rubber, motor vehicles, household appliances and mining). By 1971 this share had risen to 70%. See Barnet and Muller, *Global Reach: The Power*

of Multinational Corporations, (Simon and Schuster, New York, 1974), p. 147.

4. See Arrouda, de Souza, and Afonso, *Multinationals in Brazil*, (Latin American Research Unit, Toronto, Canada), p. 34.

5. Based on DIEESE (Inter Trade Union Department of Statistics and Socio-Economic Studies) figures quoted in Arrouda *et al, op.cit.*

6. See Sao Paulo Justice and Peace Commission, *Sao Paulo: Growth and Poverty*, (Bowerdean Press in association with Catholic Institute for International Relations, London 1978), p. 46.

7. See *Things to come: The world food crisis — the way out*, (UN World Food Conference, 1974, FAO).

8. See Susan George, *How the Other Half Dies*, (Penguin), pp. 30—31.

9. See Petras and Morley, 'US—Chile Relations and the Overthrow of the Allende Government', (mimeo, Dept. of Sociology, State University of New York at Binghampton, 1974).

10. Petras and Morley, *op.cit.* Anaconda's average rate of profit on capital in the period, 1955—70, was 20% in Chile, but only 3½% in the rest of the world. Over the same period Kennecott's profit rate was 35% in Chile, 10% in the rest of the world.

11. Admitted by William Colby, CIA Director, in testimony to the House of Representatives Armed Services Special Subcommittee on Intelligence, 22 April 1974.

12. Capitalism isn't, of course, the only system that leads to the concentration of power; it happens under a Soviet-type system too. But, on the whole, private capitalism is the 'power system' in the Third World.

13. For example, the Philippines has one of the most sophisticated cardiology units in the world. This hospital takes 50% of the total health service budget, but serves a minute proportion of the population. See C. Elliott, *Patterns of Poverty in the Third World*, (Praeger), p. 337.

14. World Bank figures quoted in S. George *op.cit.*

15. See Sao Paulo Justice and Peace Commission, *op.cit.*, p. 110: 'In effect the only kind of strike permitted by the law is that following the non-payment of wages by the firm.'

16. Recently, there have been some signs that this is beginning to happen. In May 1978 the Brazilian car industry was immobilised by the first big strike the country had seen since the military government took over in 1964. Although the strike was declared illegal, the government took no steps to repress it and the companies were forced to grant some wage increases. It's not clear why the government behaved with such unusual restraint; the military seems to be divided over the need for some measure of liberalisation. See 'Brazil, Capital and Labour in the Motor Industry', Contemporary Archive on Latin America Fact Sheet.

17. See the case study of Brazil in *Bombs for Breakfast*, (Committee on Poverty and the Arms Trade, 1978).

18. Glyn Roberts *et al., Thinking About Power,* 2nd edition, (RVA, 1978).

19. See M. Dobb, *Studies in the Development of Capitalism*, (Routledge & Kegan Paul), especially chapters 6 and 7.

2. The Road to Development

The colonial experience

In trying to decide whether Third World countries can develop along capitalist lines, the first point to consider is that the Third World has been exposed to capitalist influences for a very long time. Why didn't these influences lead to capitalist development in the Third World? The answer is obvious enough. The influence of Europe was felt because Third World countries were either European colonies or subject to colonial-type trading relationships. And, many people would say, while Europe was busily developing itself, its activities in the colonies were the source of underdevelopment there. The colonial ideology tries to persuade us that the colonial experience hastened the development of these countries, because the colonisers provided sound and just administration, an end to tribal wars, roads, railways, schools, etc. where none existed before. Opponents of this ideology argue that this is a complete caricature of the truth. The driving force behind colonialism and trade was the search for profit. The colonies were systematically underdeveloped over a period of centuries because Europe drained their wealth from them and used it for its own enrichment.

Initially this process was quite blatant, as the European powers looted and plundered precious metals from the New World. Or they took slaves from Africa and forced them to work on West Indian plantations, producing huge concentrations of wealth in the hands of the West Indian planters. But this capital was invested in Europe, not in the West Indies. In the three centuries following the 'discovery' of the New World, the flow of capital from Latin America, Africa and Asia to Europe was approximately £1,000 million, or 'more than the value of all of Europe's entire steam-driven industrial capital stock in 1800. Between 1760 and 1780 alone, Britain's income from the West and East Indies more than doubled the investment funds available for its growing industry.'[1] The drain of capital from the colonies to Europe continued right up to the end of colonial rule. For example, by the Second World War, the annual flow of wealth to Britain from both India and Malaya amounted to 10% of Indian and Malayan national income.[2]

The Europeans concentrated on producing cheap raw materials for export

19

to Europe: for example, tea, cotton and jute from India, sugar from the West Indies, copper from Zambia, cocoa from Ghana, rubber and tin from Malaya, rice from the Philippines, coffee from Brazil, rubber from Indonesia. In every case the cheapness of these goods was assured by the ruthless exploitation of labour. The chart below shows the contrast between the wealth produced by African mine workers and the wages paid to them:

Cheap Labour in the Colonies: African Mining

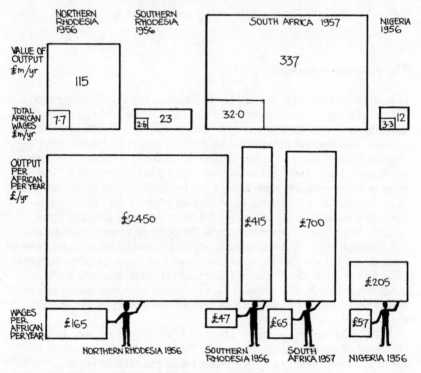

M. Barratt Brown, *After Imperialism,* (Heinemann, 1970), p.183.

Only the export sector of the colonial economy developed. The rest underdeveloped, became more backward. For example, in many colonies, village handicrafts, which could have eventually been the base for manufacturing industry, were either destroyed or failed to develop because they could not compete with the flood of cheap manufactured goods from Europe.[3] The colonisers did not find it profitable to replace these handicrafts with modern industries. Thus in India, in 1892, after more than a century of colonial rule, a minute proportion of the population was employed in modern industrial production (254,000 out of a population of 236 million).[4] Between 1891 and 1931, the proportion of the Indian population dependent on agriculture increased from 61% to 75%.[5]

Many colonies became extraordinarily dependent on exports of cash crops, as the next chart shows, and had to import food as a result:

The Economic Distortions Caused by Colonial Rule

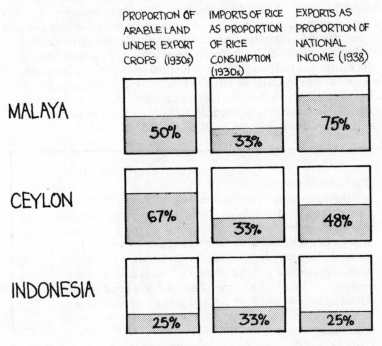

	PROPORTION OF ARABLE LAND UNDER EXPORT CROPS (1930s)	IMPORTS OF RICE AS PROPORTION OF RICE CONSUMPTION (1930s)	EXPORTS AS PROPORTION OF NATIONAL INCOME (1938)
MALAYA	50%	33%	75%
CEYLON	67%	33%	48%
INDONESIA	25%	33%	25%

M. Barratt Brown, *After Imperialism*, (Heinemann, 1970), Chapter on "The Results of Empire".

So, I would argue, the colonial experience left the colonies with an economic structure distorted to serve the needs of the European powers, not the needs of their own populations (except, of course, for the small colonial ruling class — their needs weren't neglected). Colonial Algeria is an example of the results of this process. The French took over vast areas of land in Algeria, that had previously been used for food production. They weren't interested in growing food for local consumption — it wasn't as profitable as using the land to produce wine for export. The peasants displaced from the land felt a new hunger. Although they were employed in the vineyards, their pitifully low wages did not permit them to import food from outside. Their needs had to be met by increasing the output from the land that remained in peasant agriculture. The result was exhaustion of the soil, declining productivity, and widespread malnutrition — in a word, underdevelopment.[6]

The colonial ideology refers to the advantages of European administration, education, etc. but the facts do not support this claim. European investment in infrastructure in the colonies went no further than was necessary for efficient exploitation. For example, education is often quoted as one of the benefits of European rule in Africa, but in fact education was almost non-existent for the Africans — after all, it wasn't necessary to educate unskilled labourers. Thus, in 1958, Northern Rhodesia, with enormous copper earnings every year and an African population of 2 million, possessed only one secondary school offering a complete course to the Senior Cambridge Certificate level.[7] Health services were no better: in Nigeria after 75 years of colonial rule, the British had built only one fever hospital for 30 million Nigerians, although 80% of the population suffered from malaria.[8] In Kenya, Africans were forced to pay the bulk of the taxes collected by the colonial government, but European settlers received almost all the benefit of government services (railways, roads, schools, hospitals etc.).[9]

The Colonial Crisis

'The traditional subsistence economies of Africa had provided on the whole a sufficient diet for their populations, as may be seen from the historical fact that no major part of Africa ever appears to have suffered chronic famine in the past. By 1945, however, they were far gone in ruin. Devaluation of the rural economy, coupled with the migrant labour system, and the enclosure of land by Europeans, had reached a point of continental crisis from which no colonial policy-maker could see a clear escape. Official records of the last colonial years are loud with lamentations of despair.'

(Basil Davidson, *Which Way Africa?*, Penguin.)

At this point, somebody might want to object that the argument has been over-simplified, because some colonies did develop — the outstanding example being North America; so having been a colony doesn't always lead to underdevelopment. This is true. The crucial factor in determining whether colonialism caused underdevelopment or not is the type of socio-economic structure that the colonial powers created, because some structures are much more conducive to economic development than others.[10]

In most colonies where there was abundant labour, or where it was provided through slavery, the economic system provided little incentive for investment or innovation. Labour for the plantations, haciendas and mines was extracted from the population by the use of force. When world demand rose, the easiest response for the ruling class was to squeeze more out of their workers, using force if necessary but sticking to existing economic techniques. There was no need to raise the productivity of the labour force by introducing new methods, especially when the attempt to do so required a social upheaval which could threaten the power of the existing landowners and mineowners.

The system concentrated wealth in the hands of the landowners and mineowners — not all of it drained away to Europe. But it didn't stimulate the growth of industry. It was easier for the ruling classes to spend it on luxury manufactured goods imported from Europe, or to invest it directly in European industry. This type of socio-economic structure, either created or strengthened by the colonial powers, was — and in many cases still is — a great obstacle to capitalist economic development.

To sum up: *contact with European capitalism during the colonial era caused underdevelopment rather than development not only because of the drain of capital from the colonies to Europe, but also because of the economic and social structure that was created in the colonies.* The second factor was probably the more important. It meant that the ex-colonies had a very difficult starting point from which to begin their drive for development.

This takes us on to the post-colonial era. Didn't independence give the former colonies a chance to embark on capitalist economic development and so catch up with the West? The argument, so far, suggests that capitalism in the context of colonialism underdeveloped the Third World, but it does not necessarily follow from this that the Third World countries should not try to catch up by establishing their own national capitalism. However, I want to argue that this is in fact very difficult (more difficult than it was for the old capitalist countries) and, moreover, that it involves much unnecessary suffering for the working people of the Third World (as it did for the workers of the old capitalist countries).

Post-colonial development: industrialization

Let's consider the development experience of those countries where liberation from colonial rule did not lead to socialist revolution — that is those countries where the old colonial ruling class was not destroyed economically even if their political power was reduced (as, for example, the power of the white settlers in Kenya was reduced). Many of these countries have attempted to impose capitalist economic development from on top, without changing the basic social structure. Thus they have tried to industrialize without first revolutionizing the structure of agriculture. The industrial strategy adopted by many countries was 'import substitution', i.e. setting up industries to produce the manufactured goods that were previously imported and at the same time imposing tariffs or quotas to keep imported goods out.

This strategy is a complete reversal of what happened in the mature capitalist countries. There the agricultural revolution preceded the industrial revolution. The increase in agricultural productivity provided the essential basis for the industrial revolution. It meant that food could be provided for the growing proportion of the population that worked in industry and it also meant that there was a market for industrial goods. For example, tenant farmers in England, forced to adopt the most advanced agricultural techniques in order to survive, provided a market for agricultural machinery and equipment — starting with simple tools and ending up with the combine harvester.[11]

The attempt to industrialize without these prior upheavals in agriculture has run into severe difficulties in many countries. Firstly, the imported goods now to be produced at home tended to be luxuries (e.g. cars) because the only people rich enough to import anything at all tended to be very rich. So the new industries were set up to produce these luxury goods e.g. car assembly

plants were established in many Latin American countries. But, unfortunately, this sort of industry didn't seem to lead to a self-sustaining development dynamic because the market for luxury goods was rather limited. As there hadn't been an agricultural revolution, there wasn't much demand for manufactured agricultural inputs. And, as always, the mass of the people were too poor to buy much of anything. Secondly, even if these limitations to the market were not too severe, industrialization was often hampered because the traditional agricultural sector couldn't produce enough food to support the growing urban population. Thirdly, the machinery and equipment used in the new industries tended to be imported. Since in many Third World countries exports were and are overwhelmingly agricultural (e.g. in 1970 agricultural goods accounted for over 60% of exports in 50 Third World countries)[12], new

> 'It has been calculated that the annual value of automobile production in Argentina in the mid-1960s would be sufficient to double the network of roads in that country in five years and that a much more complete system of public transportation could be provided if only part of this same amount were invested in buses and trucks instead of in private cars for the affluent minority.'
> (Andre Frank, *Lumpen-bourgeoisie, lumpen-development*.)
>
> 'Let us consider some of the implications of Latin America's highly unequal income distribution. To begin with, the half of the population which receives only 13% of the national income obviously can buy almost no durable consumer goods. 45% of the population spends only 3% of the income on consumer durables. Therefore virtually the entire output of the vastly expanded (and largely foreign owned) industrial network manufacturing automobiles, refrigerators, vacuum cleaners, etc. is destined for 5% of the population of Latin America. No wonder this industry is highly inefficient and stands half idle.' (Frank, *op.cit.*)

industries could only be set up if agricultural exports could be expanded sufficiently to pay for the necessary imports of equipment. So once again industry comes up against the barrier of an unmodernized agriculture.

Dependence on the West

This industrialization strategy hasn't been very successful at overcoming the Third World's dependence on the West. On the whole it hasn't been carried out by a new breed of Third World capitalists newly freed from colonial constraints. The new industries have tended to use the most advanced technology used in the West.[13] This technology couldn't be supplied locally, so the industrialization strategy relied on the multinationals. Although much of the capital was provided locally, the industries were owned by the multinationals, giving them the right to make all the important decisions. Their decisions are dictated by the requirements of profitability rather than by local needs. It's not profitable for them to redesign their production processes to make them appropriate to the local situation: they just move to where it's cheapest for them to use the technology they already have. Thus industry in the Third World has been capital intensive and has led to relatively slow growth in employment.[14]

National capitalists, of course, might choose the same capital intensive technology if left to themselves but at least a government that was so minded would have a better chance of controlling their activities. However, reliance

"IT'S ALL PART OF OUR POLICY TO REDUCE THE NUMBER OF UNEMPLOYED"
"ADMIRABLE MINISTER ... WHAT WILL IT PRODUCE?"
"THE NEW "RABID STOAT" ARMOURED POLICE RIOT CONTROL VEHICLE"

on the MNCs means that Third World countries are still subject to the drain of capital back to the home countries of the MNCs in the form of repatriated profits. This may often exceed the new capital provided by the multinationals to the Third World, as the example of Kenya shows (see table below): the outflow of capital was 50% greater than the inflow in the 1965–70 period.

The Drain of Capital from Kenya

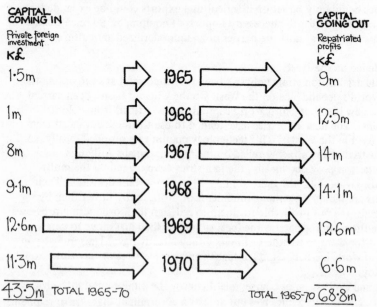

CAPITAL COMING IN		CAPITAL GOING OUT
Private foreign investment K£		Repatriated profits K£
1·5m	1965	9m
1m	1966	12·5m
8m	1967	14m
9·1m	1968	14·1m
12·6m	1969	12·6m
11·3m	1970	6·6m
43·5m TOTAL 1965–70		TOTAL 1965–70 68·8m

Adapted from C. Leys, *Underdevelopment in Kenya*, (Heinemann, 1975),

Theoretically, governments can prevent this happening by taxing MNC profits, but the government of a Third World country may be in a very weak position to do this. If taxes on profits are raised, the multinational may exploit its mobility and move its activities to another country. Moreover, multinationals have many ways of circumventing taxes on profits and exchange controls. 'Transfer pricing' is one of these technques: profits can be transferred from a Third World subsidiary to the parent multinational by overcharging the subsidiary for goods imported from the parent company. In Kenya, it is estimated that because of transfer pricing the true net capital outflow was K£40 million (or more than 50%) higher than the recorded figures for the 1964–70 period.[15] This drain of capital from Kenya was, according to Leys, enough 'to make a fairly decisive difference to the chances of an autonomous path of capitalist growth.' (*Op. cit.*, p. 138)

Western governments exert very strong pressure on Third World countries to make them 'co-operate' with the multinationals. Aid policies are used to cement economic dependence: aid projects are tied to Western firms; aid is denied to countries which have tried to control or nationalise multinational enterprises; but it flows in abundance to countries which provide tax havens for foreign companies. International lending and aid-giving institutions – the IMF, the World Bank and its offshoots – are dominated by Western governments. Their loans and aid are made conditional on the recipient country providing a climate favourable to private investment – particularly *foreign* private investment.

The table below graphically illustrates the political pattern behind much aid giving and lending.

The Politics of Western Aid

Country	Strategic political date	Increase in US and international organisation credits (%)	Increase in US aid (economic and military), and international organisation credits (%)
Brazil	1964	+180	+112
Chile	1973	+1,079	+770
Dominican Republic	1965	+305	+133
Guatemala	1954	n.a.	+5,300
Indonesia	1965	+653	+62
Iran	1953	–	+900
Philippines	1972	+171	+161
South Korea	1972	+183	–9
Uruguay	1973	+32	+21

Source: 'The US versus human rights in the Third World' by N. Chomsky and E. Herman, *Monthly Review*, July–August 1977.

In each country shown in the table, the 'strategic political date' marked a sharp move to the right, and was followed by loss of democracy and deterioration of human rights (increased use of torture and larger numbers of political prisoners, as shown by Amnesty reports). In each case, the country was made more attractive to foreign investors by easing the tax laws for foreign companies and by anti-labour measures. The table shows the change in aid and loans from the US and international organisations (World Bank, IMF) for the two or three years after the political change compared to the two or three years before the event.

The pattern is clear. *A country which opens its doors to foreign investors is rewarded with aid and loans, whatever the consequences for human rights in the country.*[16] (The only exception appears to be South Korea, but in this case the figures were greatly affected by the withdrawal of South Korean troops from South Vietnam and the resultant decline in US payments for these hired soldiers.) Aid and loans are part of the concerted effort made by the US and by international organisations to keep the Third World dependent on the West.

Thus the Third World today is just as locked into the world economic system as in colonial times. It has to export raw materials in order to be able to import machinery and equipment for its industry. But, on average, since the Second World War the price of raw materials has risen more slowly than the price of manufactures.[17] Thus the Third World has had to export an increasing proportion of its production to pay for its industrial development. The situation has been made worse for countries without oil by the quadrupling of oil prices since 1974. Many Third World countries have tried to keep up their imports of industrial equipment by borrowing more heavily from the West. As a result, they have run up enormous debts, on which they have to pay interest. According to World Bank estimates for 1974, 19 countries had a foreign public debt equal to more than 100% of their total annual exports. For 23 countries, interest payments on this debt exceeded 10% of their total export earnings.[18] There is a vicious circle here: to prevent the frustration of their development efforts caused by balance of payments problems, Third World governments are tempted to accept *more* aid, loans and foreign investment. Hence they become *more* committed to policies which meet the interests of Western governments and corporations and which prevent any shift towards self-reliant development.

Export manufactures – and achieve the New International Economic Order?
If an unmodernized agricultural sector seems to be holding up industrial expansion, then one way out might be to turn to manufacturing industrial goods for export. If it could be done, this would seem to get round all the problems mentioned above. In theory, production for export should remove the problem of limited markets and, if the traditional agricultural sector can't produce enough food to support the industrial workers, the food can be imported instead, using some of the proceeds from selling abroad. It may also be possible to modernize parts of the agricultural sector along the same lines,

e.g. by creating modern plantations and farms to produce cash crops for export.

The history of the countries that industrialized early shows the importance of expanding exports: in the period of most rapid industrialization of every, now rich, capitalist state, exports have risen as a share of the national product[19].

Some Third World countries have managed to break into world markets for manufactured goods. The most obvious examples are Hong Kong, Singapore, South Korea and Taiwan; and others are following in their footsteps (Brazil, the Philippines, Indonesia for example.) But obviously, for most Third World countries, growth through exporting is much more difficult than it was for the early industrializers, because of the now much fiercer competition in world markets: there are no longer new markets waiting to be captured as there were in the nineteenth century. Moreover, the biggest world markets for manufactures — those of the developed countries — are effectively protected from newcomers. The rich countries, on the whole, have no intention of allowing their industries to be undercut by cheap goods from the Third World.

Nevertheless, many Third World countries see the expansion of their manufactured exports as the answer to their problems. This has been a key element in the recent Third World demand for a 'new international economic order' (NIEO). Basically the Third World is demanding higher prices for its raw material exports which will then finance a new stage of industrialization based on large-scale exports of manufactured goods to the West. Hence the Third World has demanded that the rich countries open their markets to these goods. Negotiations between the rich and poor countries on the NIEO have so far failed to produce any agreement. This is not surprising. Apart from the OPEC countries since 1973, the Third World has yet to gain the power to force the West to pay more for anything. But, if an agreement were reached, the strategy could work — and maybe would lead to self-sustaining capitalist development in the Third World.

However, the costs would be high for the mass of people in these countries. Because of the need to compete with the advanced countries, labour would have to be kept cheap; so the new phase of industrialization may not do much for the standard of living of the industrial workers. Also, the strategy seems to depend on the continued import of technically advanced equipment, which suggests that the multinationals may play an even more central role than before — in other words, economic dependence may be further cemented. These two factors may have undesirable political consequences as well. Cheap labour, plus the dominant position of the multinationals, could well encourage political repression — in particular, the destruction of trade union rights. Countries may be in a position of vying for the attentions of the multinationals, and the only inducement they can offer is the cheapness and docility of their labour force. Repression seems quite a likely result.

This kind of development can be seen in those countries like Brazil, South Korea and Singapore, which are growing fastest. Perhaps these countries are in a phase analogous to the early industrial revolution phase of our own development, and possibly as their development continues they will free themselves both from political repression and from dependence on the multinationals, becoming democratic and independent centres of capitalist growth. It may be more difficult than it was for the old capitalist countries, but not impossible. On the other hand, the strategy may not work and they may relapse into continued stagnation with increasing poverty. This lies in the uncertain future. But there is no uncertainty about the costs this industrialisation strategy imposes on the working people now — in Brazil, Singapore, South Korea, Thailand, Indonesia, the Philippines; their suffering is plain for all to see. And how long will it be before their situation improves?

Modernising agriculture: the Green Revolution

I've said a lot about the failure to change the economic structure of agriculture and have suggested that governments have quailed from attempting this because of the size of the social upheavals that would be necessary. The Green Revolution has accelerated these upheavals in many countries. *It shows how a technical innovation can cause increased impoverishment for the powerless in a capitalist system.*

The Green Revolution was supposed to be brought about by the introduction of new, high-yielding varieties of wheat and rice.[20] Unfortunately, the new seeds only give of their best if they are combined with large amounts of fertiliser and water. If the whole package of seeds, fertiliser and water is not available, then the new seeds yield *less* than traditional varieties. Most peasants can't afford either to buy the fertiliser or to invest in simple irrigation, nor can they easily borrow the money to do this. The bigger landowners, on the other hand, have both reserves of their own and better access to cheap credit. They can afford the whole Green Revolution package, whereas most of the peasants can't. This situation has led to widespread evictions in Green

Revolution areas as landlords find it more profitable to farm the land themselves. What happens to the evicted peasants? Initially, they are employed on the new larger farms – the Green Revolution requires a lot of labour to spread fertiliser and water. But later, the Green Revolution areas have shown a trends towards mechanisation – tractors seem to be more profitable than people. So the landless peasants drift to join the unemployed in the urban shanty towns.

The Green Revolution has indeed led to an increase in food production and to dramatic increases in the productivity of labour and land. But the new food surpluses haven't meant more to eat for the hungry, because they've no money to buy it. Even in Mexico, the home of the Green Revolution, one study [21] concluded that there was little reason to believe that the Green Revolution had helped to increase per capita food consumption. Most of the extra production was exported – and the profits went to the large landowners.

The Green Revolution has political consequences. The peasants haven't always given up without a struggle. In India and Pakistan, for example, there have been violent incidents as peasants were ejected from their land.[22] As the Green Revolution spreads, the struggle will become more intense and the ruling class's response is likely to be political repression. In India, large landowners dominate most of the regional assemblies. Hence they are in a good position to use state power to combat peasant resistance to eviction. This may lie behind the large increases there have been, particularly in the early seventies, in the Indian police and security force budgets – necessary, according to the government, because there have been riots over food shortages and 'communal and political disputes'. Coupled with the loss of democratic rights under Mrs. Gandhi's government, this suggests that the Indian ruling class has responded in the predicted way. It remains to be seen whether the change of government will make much difference.

If the Green Revolution continues in this way, it can only lead to the destruction of peasant society and its replacement by large-scale capitalist agriculture. The human suffering caused by the process is intense. It is, of course, not just a matter of technology: it is technology combined with private control of land that causes the problem. If the 'free' land market is controlled by a land reform, the Green Revolution need not cause impoverishment and may even benefit the peasants.

To recap the argument so far:

(1) Following the road to development taken by the rich countries means pursuing a capitalist economic development strategy.

(2) Contrary to conventional wisdom, this is considerably more, rather than less, difficult for late starters. Firstly, most of the late starters have a social and economic structure distorted by colonialism and this hardly provides a favourable starting point for development. Moreover, political independence has not brought economic independence. Most countries have been unable to avoid reliance on the multinationals for their industrialisation. Secondly, countries attempting to sell in world markets have to face intense competition and restrictive trade practices from advanced economies – a

problem which the rich countries either never had to face (Britain) or had to do to a much lesser extent. The need to compete dictates an economic development strategy − in industry and agriculture − based on cheap labour, possibly combined with political repression to ensure that labour remains cheap.

(3) *Hence there is no easy route to capitalist industrialisation, nor is there any way of avoiding the social upheavals and suffering associated with the capitalist modernisation of agriculture.* Thus, even in those countries that succeed in developing along capitalist lines, the benefits from capitalist development, both economic and political, are likely to be long delayed for the mass of people in the Third World. Their standard of living may even get worse first. (e.g. peasants who become landless as a result of the Green Revolution).

The Socialist Road

If the capitalist road to development is rejected, what alternative is there? Continued stagnation is one possibility, but this has its own massive toll of suffering. The other possibility is some form of socialist revolution. But, somebody will surely object, socialist economic development may cause even more suffering than capitalist development. In any country, capitalist or socialist, breaking out of underdevelopment means raising the rate of investment massively, in both agriculture and industry. The rate of investment can only be raised if society is somehow induced or forced to save more and consume less. Some would argue that this process may be even more painful under socialism than under capitalism because socialist governments may be more efficient at extracting savings out of the population.

Stalinist development
The history of the Soviet Union gives some support to this view. Determined to industrialise rapidly, and faced with the unwillingness of the richer peasantry to supply their surplus to the towns (the rest of the peasantry had no surplus to supply), Stalin resorted to overwhelming physical force. Collectivisation was conceived to be the mechanism for squeezing more out of agriculture. In one year (1929−30) half of all Russian farms were collectivised − at the point of a gun. The richer peasants (kulaks) were liquidated. Masses of people were killed, deported to remote unpopulated lands in Siberia, or imprisoned in forced labour camps. Nothing was allowed to stand in the way of industrialisation: Russia continued to export grain even in the famines of the early thirties in order to continue the import of machinery for industry. Political repression of the inevitable opposition to this ruthless modernisation was efficient and brutal.

Socialism without repression?
If this is revolution, is it worth having? True, it raised Russia to the rank of

industrial superpower within 20 years. The standard of living has risen greatly, and there has been some relaxation of repression since Stalin's day. But the cost of modernisation has been enormous. However, I don't think this is the inevitable outcome of socialist revolution. Other revolutionary regimes have not attempted to industrialise so fast and hence have not attempted a Stalinist squeeze of agriculture. They have nevertheless achieved significant economic growth and improvements in mass living standards.

In both China and Cuba, for example, the revolution was based far more on the support of the peasantry than was the case in Russia.[23] As a result, the leadership in both countries has always made greater efforts to keep this support in its attempts to revolutionise agriculture. Thus, in both countries, collectivisation of agriculture was achieved without the violence seen in the Russian campaign against the kulaks. In China, the government moved step by step towards collectivisation, using persuasion and material inducements rather than force, e.g. attempts were made to ensure that the richer peasants did not lose by joining co-operatives and to persuade the rest that their incomes would be raised. China began by attempting a Soviet-style rapid industrialisation, but abandoned this as the costs of neglecting agriculture and of forcing the pace generally were realised. The leadership was flexible enough to learn from its mistakes and not to press on ruthlessly with an 'industrialise at all costs' strategy as in Russia in the thirties.

However, economic growth in China has been rapid — and, unlike fast growing capitalist Third World countries, this growth has been combined with equity. From 1952 to 1974 economic growth averaged about 6% p.a., while per capita growth was about 4% p.a. In India, by contrast, per capita growth was only 1% p.a. over the same period. Chinese agricultural output has grown more slowly, at about the same rate as population — 2% p.a.[24] This is still a considerable achievement, given that China suffers from a severe land shortage — China feeds a quarter of the world's population on only 7% of the world's cultivated area. It has attempted to make up for the shortage of land by mobilising its vast population to improve the soil and to work it more intensively (e.g. through irrigation works and double-cropping).

The policy of rural industrialisation has also helped absorb surplus agricultural labour. Small- to medium-scale industries have been established in rural areas, with the primary aim of supporting the modernisation of agriculture (e.g. they make nearly all farm tools and much simple farm machinery). Thus China has prevented the chronic unemployment, and reduced the underemployment in rural areas, that is a feature of so many Third World capitalist countries.

China is not a completely egalitarian society. Significant income differentials still exist though, of course, they are very much lower than in capitalist Third World countries. Eckstein found that the most senior staff in a Chinese factory were paid up to 20 times as much as the lowest paid apprentice. In the US, the ratio is 50 to 1, whereas in some African countries managers are paid 80 times as much as unskilled workers. However, these figures for China understate the degree of equality there compared to other countries, because they take no account of China's egalitarian distribution of basic goods.

Necessities — food, housing, clothing, health and education — are either free or very cheap, and rationed. Those who earn higher incomes can spend them on the very expensive luxury goods, but they can't use them to get more than their fair share of scarce necessities. China remains a poor country, but it has ensured a basic minimum standard of living for all. The contrast, both with pre-revolutionary China and other Third World countries, could not be greater.

I'm not trying to argue that the Chinese regime is ideal. Like other socialist states, it is authoritarian and undemocratic, even if it allows more popular participation than most. But there never was a democratic alternative in China, and this is probably true of most Third World countries today. The choice is between a capitalist or communist one party state. *And, unpalatable though it may be, I think we have to choose whether to support socialist or capitalist development in the Third World — we're not justified in refusing to take sides.* Western governments and multinational companies are not hindered by any worries about democracy from supporting capitalist dictatorships. They make great efforts to subvert other, apparently socialist governments. And they have shown themselves ready to crush democratic attempts at socialist revolution (Chile). If we refuse to choose between the two sides, are we not giving our tacit consent to these policies?

Notes and References

1. A.G. Frank, *Capitalism and Underdevelopment in Latin America*, (Penguin, 1971) pp. 311−2.
2. M. Barratt Brown, *After Imperialism*, (Heinemann, 1970), chapter on 'The Results of Empire'.
3. See for example articles on the effects of British colonial rule on the Indian economy in B. Chandra (ed.), *The Indian Economy in the 19th Century − a Symposium*, (Indian Economic and Social History Association, Delhi School of Economics, 1969).
4. *Ibid.*
5. M. Barratt Brown, *op. cit.*
6. See B. Davidson, *Which Way Africa?*, (Penguin, 1967), p. 39.
7. *Ibid*, p. 44.
8. See M. Barratt Brown, *op.cit.*, p. 170.
9. See C. Leys, *Underdevelopment in Kenya*, (Heinemann, 1975), Chapter 2.
10. See R. Brenner, 'The Origins of Capitalist Development', *New Left Review*, 104, 1977.
11. See Samir Amin, 'The New International Economic Order', *Monthly Review*, July−August, 1977. Also M. Dobb, *op.cit.*
12. See K. Morton and P. Tulloch, *Trade and Developing Countries*, (ODI, Croom Helm, 1977).
13. See R. Sutcliffe, *Industry and Under-Development*, (Addison-Wesley, 1971), p. 268.
14. Between 1963 and 1965, manufacturing production in developing countries grew by 6.9% p.a., but manufacturing employment grew by only 4.7% p.a. (*UN Yearbook of Industrial Statistics 1975* Vol. 1.) In some countries the situation was much worse. For example, in Kenya between 1964 and 1969, output in the non-agricultural sector rose by 10% p.a. while private non-agricultural employment grew by only 2% p.a., less than the population growth rate of 3% p.a. (See C. Leys, *op.cit.*, p. 138.)
15. See C. Leys, *op.cit.*, p. 138.
16. Deflating the figures to remove the trend increase in aid and loans does not alter these findings.
17. The Declining Terms of Trade* between raw materials and manufactures.

	Agriculture	Metals minerals & ores	34 commodities (excl. petroleum)
1950−54	108	85	103
1955−59	95	88	93
1960−64	81	78	80
1965−69	78	100	83
1970−74	83	85	83

Source: Commodities and Export Projections Division, World Bank.
*Defined as index of raw materials prices in US $ weighted by values of exports from developing countries (in 1967) divided by an index of the US $ prices of exports of manufactures from developed countries to all destinations.

18. M. Abdel-Fadil, F. Cripps, J. Wells, 'A New International Economic Order?' *Cambridge Journal of Economics*, June 1977.
19. See M. Barratt-Brown, *The Economics of Imperialism*, (Penguin, 1974), p. 111.
20. See the chapter on the Green Revolution in Susan George, *How the Other Half Dies*, (Penguin, 1976).
21. Cynthia de Alcantara, 'Modernisation without Development: Patterns of Agricultural Policy and Rural Change in the Birthplace of the Green Revolution', in *Social and Economic Implications of large-scale Introduction of New Varieties of Foodgrain*, (UN Research Institute for Social Development, 1974).
22. See S. George, *op.cit.*, pp. 128–9.
23. For China, see A. Eckstein, *China's Economic Revolution*, (Cambridge University Press). For Cuba, see L. Huberman and P. Sweezy, *Socialism in Cuba*, (Monthly Review Press, 1969) and R. Dumont, *Is Cuba Socialist?* (Deutsch, 1974).
24. Eckstein, *op.cit.*

3. Strategies for Change I: Development Action

If, as I've argued, development is about power, is there anything concerned people in the West can do directly for the Third World? If true development requires a political struggle, a struggle by the poor of the Third World to wrest power from the elite, does that mean that there is little people outside the Third World can contribute — because 'people must make their own revolutions'? Or is there a role for 'Third World activists' in the West?

Clearly, many people think there is a role, as witnessed by the large number of voluntary groups engaged in some kind of 'action for development' in this country. Should the concerned individual join one of them — and if so, which one? That's a question which people will have to answer for themselves, but I think it is useful to look at the development groups and assess their 'strategy for change' in the light of the approach to development outlined in the first two chapters.

There seem to me to be two types of strategy people in the West can follow to work towards change in the Third World. Firstly, they can *provide resources* — money, goods and skilled people — to the Third World. Secondly, they can attempt to *change the policies and behaviour of Western institutions* (governments, companies, trade unions, churches, voluntary organisations) towards the Third World.

Resources for the Third World

Groups[1] which follow the first strategy — provision of resources — range from liberation solidarity movements on the one hand, to volunteer sending organisations and fundraising charities on the other. Their only common characteristic is the activity of collecting and sending resources overseas. Everything else — destination of the aid, its expected results, the general · political perspective — obviously varies widely over this spectrum of groups.

If we accept a political view of development, how should we regard the activity of collecting and sending relatively small amounts of resources (money and/or people) to the Third World? The liberation support movements generally share this political approach to development and 'resource aid' is usually only a small part of their activities. Most are heavily involved in the second strategy, particularly in attempts to influence public opinion on, and hence government policy towards, the countries of their concern. So, if you participate in one of these groups, you'll be involved in both types of strategy.

What about the 'mainstream' charities and development agencies (Save the Children, Action in Distress, Christian Aid, Oxfam, War on Want, the volunteer sending organisations): how do their activities fit into our approach?

Their standard justification is that, even though their aid makes very little difference to world poverty overall, it may make a huge difference to some individuals' lives — the difference between life and death in some cases. Even recognising that the solution to poverty requires fundamental social and economic changes doesn't necessarily mean that we shouldn't do what we can to help people *now*; after all, they may be dead before fundamental change is achieved. Hence we are urged to give generously both for immediate relief — 'if you help, this child will be fed, these old people will be sheltered' — and for development projects — 'if you help, this village will have a well, these farmers will have better ploughs'. If your next door neighbour was starving, you wouldn't refuse to help on the grounds that poverty can't be solved by individual action alone. So why should it be any different when, instead of your next door neighbour, the starving are thousands of miles away overseas? Why should mere geographical distance change one's attitudes?

Put like this, there seems to be no question about the rightness of contributing to Third World charities, etc. But problems arise when 'helping' in this way appears to *conflict* with the aim of achieving fundamental change. And this, of course, leads to the question: how *is* fundamental change going to be achieved? I can't pretend to have solved all the political problems raised here, but I think we can be confident that the solution to world poverty will require political struggles both in the Third World and in the West. On that basis we can identify some *minimum* requirements which the charities should meet, without first having to provide a detailed 'blueprint' for fundamental change. I think there are at least two of these minimum requirements:

(1) In the Third World, aid should, at the very least, not strengthen the existing power structure, and in most cases should be given in a way that advances the awareness and organisation of the poor and oppressed, increasing their ability to fight against the forces that oppress them.

(2) In the West, fundraising activities shouldn't be at the expense of educating people about the true causes of world poverty. Propaganda shouldn't allow people to think that charity is a solution — in particular, it should make people realise the Western power structure's *responsibility* for supporting and creating poverty-creating social systems in the Third World.

Assessing the charities

Let's consider the charities and the British volunteer programme in the light of these requirements — and with the aim of seeing what the aware individual can do. I'm not going to try and present a thorough survey of the field, but make a few points which are relevant (I think) in deciding which agency to

support. Firstly, agencies which stress an 'apolitical' stance are very un-
likely to meet these requirements. Of the main fundraising agencies, only
War on Want would accept the political view of development outlined above.
The others range along a continuum with the child welfare agencies (Save the
Children, Action in Distress) at the conservative 'apolitical' end while Christian
Aid and Oxfam are closer to War on Want. Of the volunteer sending organisa-
tions, VSO is 'apolitical' while the smaller agencies — UNAIS, IVS, CIIR —
are much more aware of the political implications of their activities.[2]

I think the 'apolitical' stance is a trap and a mystification, because it's
impossible to be apolitical. Its apologists say that their function is to
respond to *need*, without regard to political or religious criteria. Aid agencies
must be impartial, they say, for what right have we in the West to impose our
own political priorities on the Third World? Of course, we should avoid
paternalism and interference — but does that mean we must avoid *any* kind of
choice between social and political forces in the Third World? I don't think
it's even possible to avoid the choice: *any* aid project will help some groups
more than others and will therefore affect the distribution of income and
power. 'Apolitical' agencies are making implicit political choices all the time
as they decide which projects to support. VSO, for example, responds to
government requests for volunteers. In repressive Third World countries
(e.g. Thailand, Indonesia), this certainly isn't seen as non-political behaviour

by the governments' radical political opponents. It is seen as support for the *status quo* – and therefore it won't meet our first requirement. Perhaps it's not possible to place volunteers in these countries except through the government. In that case, I would argue that no volunteers should be sent. The number of volunteers shouldn't be an end in itself. Unlike VSO, the small volunteer agencies, particularly CIIR, have worked towards a more radical concept of volunteering – and have accepted a much reduced programme as a result.

Another 'apolitical' agency is the charity, Action in Distress. This charity arranges 'postal adoption' of children in the Third World: individuals in Britain are urged to sponsor a child, providing a regular weekly contribution towards the child's nutrition, health, education, etc. It's hard to see how this kind of activity can meet the requirement that aid should increase the power of the poor in the Third World. By giving only to children in this very individualistic way, its funds cannot possibly be used collectively by organised groups of the underprivileged. Moreover, the whole concept of relief via adoption creates dependence of children and their families on donors in the West – and therefore both mirrors and strengthens the existing power structure in which the Third World as a whole is dependent on the West.

At the other end of the spectrum, War on Want sends aid to liberation movements in Zimbabwe, Namibia, South Africa and Eritrea. This obviously meets the requirement of challenging the existing power structure. War on Want seems to be willing to make a political choice. For example, it argues that black Zimbabweans can either '*accept* economic exploitation, dehumanising restrictions and the degradations of racist rule' or they can '*struggle* for equality and majority rule, for the right to determine their own future and to control and share their own resources. War on Want supports those who have chosen to struggle.'[3] In general, War on Want's philosophy stresses the need to 'ensure that our actions do not increase the dependence of underdeveloped countries on the industrial world and reinforce economic and political inequality between and within these countries.'[4] Therefore War on Want has 'chosen to work with groups of the organised poor', even if this leads to conflict with the power holders in Third World countries.

Oxfam is considerably less explicit, and more ambiguous, than this about the political content of its work. In 'The Oxfam Year' for 1974/75 it was said in a statement of objectives that 'we can act as a small-scale *socialist* catalyst; helping and encouraging people to realize their full potential; helping small groups to become self-reliant and to *combat the oppressive factors in their environment.*' (emphasis added). But in the 1976/77 review there seemed to be some back-tracking: 'Oxfam is having to assess the social and economic structures in which poor farmers and others are forced to live, and to seek ways in which they can be encouraged to react to those conditions. This is a tremendous challenge to us but we are sure that it is one from which we must not shrink.'

'Seeking ways in which poor people can be encouraged to react to social and economic conditions' seems less militant than 'helping small groups . . .

combat the oppressive factors in their environment'. From their public statements, it seems that the policy of helping small groups did not and does not extend to helping liberation movements. Moreover, Oxfam does not seem to favour countries like Angola, Guinea-Bissau, Mozambique and Vietnam where socialist revolution has taken place:

Oxfam Grants, 1976-77

TOTAL GRANTS 1976/7		AMOUNTS IN £ AND PERCENTAGE OF TOTAL		
		OTHER COUNTRIES		
INDIA 787,000 (16·9%)		ANGOLA, GUINEA-BISSAU MOZAMBIQUE, VIETNAM }70,000 (1·5%)		
		TANZANIA 270,000 (6%)		
	BRAZIL 381,000 (8·2%)	BANGLADESH 315,000 (6·8%)	S. AFRICA 32000 (0·7%) ZIMBABWE 83000 (1·8%) INDONESIA 174,000 (3·7%)	

J. Briscoe, 'Improving Health Care Where Health is Underdeveloped', unpublished paper commissioned by Oxfam, Dacca, 1978.

Oxfam might argue that its larger grants to Brazil, Indonesia, Bangladesh and India merely reflect the much larger populations of those countries compared to the socialist countries. But how possible is it in such countries to 'help small groups to become self-reliant and to combat the oppressive factors in their environment'? Briscoe's study suggests that, in Bangladesh at least, Oxfam cannot and does not live up to these principles.[5] For example, 85% of Oxfam's 1976/77 health grant (54% of the total) to Bangladesh was used for the construction, servicing and maintenance of Oxfam sanitation units in bustee and Bihari camps. There is no local participation in the construction or maintenance of these units. Only 10% of the health grant went to Bangladeshi organisations. 78% of the total went to the Irish charity, Concern, an organisation which, according to Briscoe, has shown 'virtually no interest in involving local people in the planning of its projects'.[6] Perhaps Oxfam supports Concern because it cannot find enough Bangladeshi-run organisations of the right type, i.e. which involve the poor in the struggle to improve their own lives. But in this case its relative neglect of the socialist countries is harder to understand — for surely, in these countries, where mass-based revolutions have occurred, it must be far easier than in Bangladesh, Brazil, Indonesia etc. to find locally-run organisations worthy of support?

Certainly some of Oxfam's projects do help the poor gain more control over their own lives, and therefore do satisfy our first requirement (e.g. aid to an agricultural co-operative to build a processing factory and to buy transport, so helping the co-operative control its own marketing and eliminate the middle-man). But, if the example of Bangladesh is anything to go by, such projects may be a rather small proportion of the total.

Fundraising versus the truth about world poverty

What about the second requirement: that fundraising activities shouldn't create, or strengthen, false views on the causes of world poverty? Here I can do no better than quote from Jørgen Lissner's book, *The Politics of Altruism: the political behaviour of voluntary development agencies.*[7] After reading 'thousands' of voluntary development agency publications in several languages, Lissner concluded that 'it was a plausible hypothesis' that the 'one lasting image coming across to the public from the mainstream agencies is this: 'the development problem is all out there. It is caused by indigenous factors inside the low-income countries . . . our present standard of living is the result of our own efforts alone. The only, or most important, thing we can do to reduce poverty and human suffering in the Third World is to provide more aid resources.'

Lissner found that the agencies either: (a) ascribe Third World poverty to hostile forces of nature beyond human control, e.g. natural disasters such as drought, flood, earthquake; or (b) give no indication of the causes of poverty; or (c) suggest the 'vicious circle' hypothesis: people remain poor because they are poor — and hence uneducated, undernourished, unhealthy, technologically backward. When the rich world was mentioned, it was blamed for its selfish affluence and for allowing Third World poverty to *continue*, but not for having caused or aggravated poverty in the first place. War on Want and Oxfam-Canada were the only agencies studied by Lissner which gave a more radical view of development. Thus Lissner concludes that most agency propaganda has two very important results: (a) *people in the rich countries are exonerated from any responsibility for poverty in the Third World; and* (b) *the belief is instilled that, on the whole, the developed countries are generous and high-minded towards the Third World.* There is also a third important result not mentioned by Lissner: *the agencies create the impression that poor people in the Third World are passive, doing nothing but waiting for us to help them.*

In other words, Lissner found that most agencies fail to satisfy the second requirement. They give a distorted or false picture of Third World poverty and development. Why? In the more conservative agencies, such as those dealing with child welfare, their propaganda probably reflects their views accurately. But, in many others, people are probably aware that their propaganda presents at least an incomplete picture. Their justification is neatly put by Lissner. 'We would immediately antagonise and alienate a significant part of our constituency, if we came out asserting that the First World enriches itself at the expense of the Third World. Many people would simply stop supporting us financially. What's the point of having morally clean but

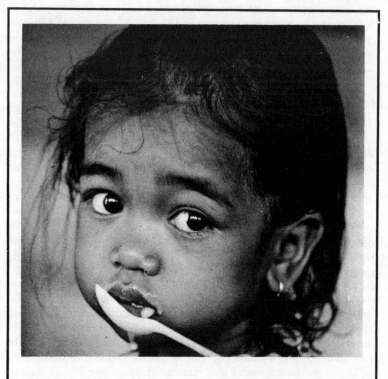

The appeal:
'Save the Children — does it make any difference?
'Yes it does! There will always be children in need. But
over the 58 years that Save the Children has been working,
there has also been a steady chain of successes: hundreds of
thousands of children helped, fed, made well, educated,
projects handed over to communities that can now run
them themselves . . .' (*Save the Children* brochure.)
The message:
Poverty is inevitable, a fact of life rather than a result of
unjust social and economic structures. Poor people depend
on us, not only for money but also to teach them how to
look after themselves.

financially empty hands? The important thing is to raise funds so that we can
support worthwhile activities in the Third World. *Others* will have to tell the
unpleasant truths.'

This education or truth by proxy seems to be the strategy followed by the
biggest British agencies — namely Oxfam and Christian Aid. Although both

these agencies have their own development education departments, they support separate groups or institutions to do the *controversial* educational work for them. Both the World Development Movement (WDM) and the *New Internationalist* were set up with the backing of Oxfam and Christian Aid (though WDM became independent when the agencies' support for it got them into trouble with the Charity Commissioners.) Both of these proxies put forward a considerably more radical view of development than Oxfam or Christian Aid, e.g. neither hesitates to lay some responsibility for causing Third World poverty at the door of the First World. By contrast, Oxfam's main paper, *Oxfam News*, concentrates on individual projects in the Third World and on fundraising activities in Britain. The problems of development are rarely put in a wider context. In other words, *Oxfam News* generally refrains from 'telling the unpleasant truths'.

But backing more radical groups is hardly a solution to the educational problem since the conservative part of Oxfam's and Christian Aid's constituency is probably not reached by the WDM or the *New Internationalist*. Their more conservative supporters will only be reached by Oxfam and Christian Aid themselves. Does the need for cash justify not educating these supporters on the causes of world poverty? If you believe that these groups, by suggesting that charity is the answer, indirectly help to perpetuate the world economic system, then the answer is probably 'no'. They may help in the short run, but in the long run they may do more harm than good. Moreover, War on Want's experience suggests that provided a professional job is done on promoting the new policies, fears of losing funds may be over-stated: following their adoption of a more radical political stance in 1973, the public responded with increased support (see War on Want's Annual Report for 1973–74).

These criticisms of Oxfam and Christian Aid aren't meant to suggest that we should boycott them. I don't want to deny that much of what they do in the Third World is valuable. But the criticisms do suggest that there is a role for *critical* supporters. Since these agencies influence a large number of people, they have the potential for significantly affecting public attitudes towards the Third World. Thus it is important for critical supporters to work within these agencies for a more radical development education policy. Whether there is any possibility for changing, from within, the activities of the most fervently apolitical charities (Save the Children and Action in Distress) is another matter. 'Reform from Within' is only a feasible tactic if there is a possibility of forming a ginger group within the organisation. But the further the organisation is from what you consider to be right, the more likely you are to be isolated and ineffective. Criticism from outside may then be the best approach.

Similar problems arise with the British Volunteer Programme (BVP).[8] The smaller agencies are generally sympathetic to the view of development espoused here and hence there is scope for constructive co-operation and, if necessary, criticism. But with VSO's policy makers it is another matter. Should returned volunteers (RVs) work within the BVP structure in the hope of changing VSO policy, or should they call for VSO's abolition, as incapable of reform? Returned Volunteer Action (RVA) has chosen the former course being moderate and reformist rather than aggressive, in the hope of reaching sympathetic people within VSO. And VSO has made some changes, possibly as a result of pressure from RVA amongst others, e.g. VSO decided to appoint field officers, and recognised the need for an evaluation of the British Volunteer Programme.[9] However, fundamentally, VSO's concept of volunteering remains unchanged. VSO does not see volunteering as a means of helping the underprivileged challenge the power structure, of providing resources to the 'organised poor'. It continues to support elitist education systems with volunteers. Hence concerned returned volunteers should continually assess and re-assess the potential of a reformist approach towards, as opposed to an explicit attack on, VSO.

Getting the West 'off their backs'

The second strategy for the elimination of Third World poverty that can be adopted by concerned people in the West is more obviously political. It starts from the premise that the *Western power structure is partly responsible for the political and economic mechanisms that create and perpetuate poverty in the Third World*. The strategy is then to try to persuade/cajole/force Western institutions to change their behaviour towards or in the Third World. Also, solidarity action can be taken by workers in multinational companies. Thus campaigns are directed at *governments*, on their aid and trade policies, their collaboration with anti-developmental regimes; and at *multinational companies*, on their exploitation of Third World workers, on their creation of dependence in the Third World, on their abuse of monopoly power by over-pricing, tax avoidance, and controlling access to technology in Third World countries. Even if all these campaigns in the West were successful, they wouldn't eliminate poverty and injustice in the Third World — there'd still be the necessity for internal political revolutions. But if we feel that we in the West can do little to encourage the latter process, it's still worth working to give Third World people a chance by 'getting the West off their backs', and perhaps weakening their own elites in the process.

As far as transferring resources to the Third World is concerned, the potential of such campaigns is much greater than that of fundraising campaigns, just because governments and multinationals control vast amounts of resources, while fundraising campaigns are basically aimed at individuals. Thus Oxfam, for example, raises around £7 million a year, while the British aid programme runs at around £400 million a year. A campaign to get at least some British aid given to support the 'organised poor' in the Third World could, if successful, be a great deal more effective than a fundraising effort to add to — say — War on Want's support for the organised poor.

But probably most campaigns are not successful, in the sense that the institutions attacked change their policies. The campaigns may still be worth conducting for the less obvious benefit of influencing public opinion, raising public consciousness in general on the *causes* of world poverty, even if their specific objectives are not met. Unfortunately for participants in these campaigns, they can't be sure whether public consciousness has been raised or not, so it's easy to become disillusioned. Fundraising campaigns, even if more limited in scope, do at least have tangible, quantifiable results, so that people can see what they've achieved.

There are a large number of groups following this strategy, ranging from liberation support movements, whose aims are obviously political, to groups like the World Development Movement, War on Want, the Haslemere Group, Third World First, which tend to concentrate more on economic issues (aid, trade, multinationals). Two examples will be given here.

Campaigning against the 'Baby Killer'

Firstly, let's look at the campaign on the baby foods issue, (see Chapter I for explanation of the issue). The campaign was launched by the *New Internationalist* in 1973, after the appearance of the UN's Protein Advisory Group report on the dangers of bottle-feeding. It was taken up by War on Want with the publication of its booklet, *The Baby Killer*, which blamed the baby food companies for promoting bottle-feeding, despite the dangers in the Third World. The baby foods campaign then became international.[10] Two Swiss development groups translated *The Baby Killer* into German under the title *Nestle Kills Babies*. Nestle sued them for criminal libel and won (having dropped two of its three charges), but it lost in the sense that it received a great deal of unfavourable publicity. The issue was also taken up in the United States, where a co-ordinated campaign has been spear-headed by the New York based Interfaith Center for Corporate Responsibility.

On May 23, 1978, Senator Edward Kennedy's Subcommittee on Health and Scientific Research conducted a hearing on the promotion and marketing of baby foods in the Third World. Dr. Oswaldo Ballarin, president and chairman of Nestle Brazil, testified on behalf of Nestle:

Dr. Ballarin: United States Nestle Company has advised me that their research indicates that this (the campaign to halt the promotion of baby foods in the Third World) is actually an indirect attack on the free world's economic system. A worldwide church organisation, with its stated purpose of undermining the free enterprise system, is at the forefront of these activities.

Senator Kennedy: . . . We've heard the testimony of probably nine different witnesses. It seemed to me that they were expressing a very deep compassion and concern about the well-being of infants, the most vulnerable people on the face of this world. Would you agree with me that your product should not be used where there is impure water?

Dr. Ballarin: Of course not; but we cannot cope with that.

Senator Kennedy: . . . What do you feel is your corporate responsibility to find out the extent of the use of your product in those circumstances in the developing part of the world? Do you feel that you have any responsibility?

Dr. Ballarin: We can't take that responsibility, sir.

Quoted in *Multinational Monitor,* Winter 1978–79, p. 12.

The baby foods companies have made some changes in an effort to head off further criticism. They have begun to draw up their own codes of conduct regulating marketing practices in the Third World. One company has even agreed to spend $100,000 promoting the value of breast milk. But the campaign is not just about marketing practices. The critics regard baby foods as the equivalent of a dangerous drug. They argue that it should only be distributed free and under medical supervision. Unsurprisingly the companies have shown no sign of accepting this. If their activities are to be controlled in this more fundamental sense, Third World governments will have to impose regulations on them.

So far only Algeria seems likely to do this, by putting baby foods under state control. However, other governments have taken more limited action. Sweden, Papua New Guinea and Guinea-Bissau have banned all direct advertising of baby foods. The overseas development ministries in the UK and the Netherlands have begun a 'critical evaluation' of milk aid policies. The US Congress passed an amendment to the International Development and Food Assistance Act requiring a strategy to promote breast-feeding to be drawn up.

As the largest disburser of food aid, this American action is significant.

The achievements of the campaign so far are important. More ethical marketing practices and a change in milk aid policies may slow down (or even reverse) the spread of bottle feeding in the Third World. This may already have saved more lives and prevented more malnutrition than a campaign of similar scale to raise funds for child care in the Third World. But the campaign is still far from achieving its more fundamental objectives.

Campaigning against apartheid

The second example is the network of campaigns on South Africa. The case of South Africa is very important for two main reasons. Firstly, it illustrates very well the *political nature of true development: that development is not just a matter of increasing production.* South Africa is well endowed with natural resources and now has a significant mining and manufacturing sector. Average income per head is quite high at $1,272 per annum in 1974 (World Bank figures), thus qualifying South Africa as a semi-developed country. But, despite the overall wealth of the country, the black majority (80% of the population) live in severe poverty. The extent of South Africa's inequality is starkly shown by malnutrition and infant mortality figures:

Health Indicators by Race in South Africa

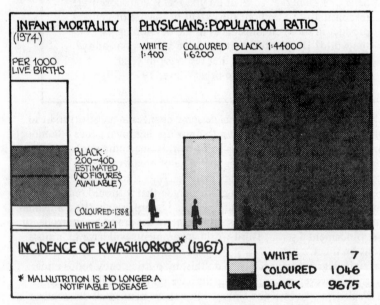

Dr. J. Le Fanu, "Notes on Health Care and Apartheid in South Africa", document prepared for Anti-Apartheid Conference, "Apartheid or Health", 1979.

Blacks are debarred by racist laws from sharing in South Africa's wealth. The whites' privileged position rests on the brutal exploitation of the black labour force. Since the whites cannot be dislodged, except by force, development for the blacks is clearly overwhelmingly a political problem. Because of the ultra-exploitative nature of the white supremacist state, any form of black rule can hardly fail to improve the standard of living of the black majority.

Secondly, South Africa is important because it is a very clear example of *the responsibility of the Western powers for preserving an unjust, poverty-creating system*. The South African boom of the sixties was made possible by massive inflows of capital from the West, particularly from Britain. By the end of 1973 the total direct foreign investment in South Africa was £3,585 million, of which UK based corporations accounted for £2,150 million.[11] More recently, US and European banks have provided the finance for South African investment, replacing direct investment which has been reduced by political worries, especially since Soweto. The loans have helped finance a huge increase in defence expenditure and massive state investment in steel and energy, essential to the siege economy that the South African government intends to create.

Apologists for the investors claim that, by investing in South Africa, they are helping to promote economic development which will gradually whittle away apartheid. But there is no evidence that economic development so far has had this effect. And this is not surprising, since it is the apartheid system

which promotes the profitability of investment, and hence economic development by guaranteeing cheap labour. So Britain's economic stake in South Africa makes her a partner in apartheid. British complicity creates the opportunity for successful campaigns to have a significant political effect in South Africa, but also makes success harder to achieve because of the powerful groups in Britain with a vested interest in the continuation of apartheid.

The Anti-Apartheid Movement (AAM) is the main campaigning group in Britain on South Africa. The campaigns are basically designed to achieve the economic and political isolation of South Africa. They are aimed: (1) at governments — urging legislation to strengthen the arms embargo and to secure an immediate freeze on loans and investment as a prelude to British withdrawal and the imposition of all-embracing economic sanctions; (2) at companies and banks — urging an end to loans and investment (particularly in industries which augment South Africa's military capacity), recognition of black trade unions, and higher black wages; (3) at shareholding institutions — urging them to sell their shares in UK companies with interests in South Africa; (4) at sports and the arts — urging a sports and cultural boycott; (5) at consumers — urging a boycott of South African goods and of banks with major interests in South Africa.

Methods used in the campaign are wide-ranging. [12] The AAM and other allied organisations put out a steady stream of publications designed to influence public opinion. Quite large numbers of people are mobilised for demonstrations, pickets, leafleting, meetings, boycotts. A network of local and student groups across the country helps to organise these activities. Campaigners put pressure directly on the government by getting sympathetic MPs to ask questions in Parliament and to write letters to ministers. Offending companies are reached through shareholders' meetings — campaigners become shareholders, thus gaining the right to speak at these meetings. Increasingly, the AAM has been trying to win support within the trade unions, in the hope that unions can be persuaded to use their industrial power against South Africa — for example, by blacking goods intended for South Africa. The problem here is to create solidarity between British and African workers which will overcome the immediate conflict of interest between them, i.e. if unions black South African goods and British firms lose orders as a result, some workers will lose their jobs. The campaign has tried to persuade workers, with some success, that the existence of a pool of cheap labour in South Africa is a greater long-term threat to their jobs, since multinationals may switch operations from Britain to South Africa.

Some limited successes have been achieved. For example, several universities and church organisations have been persuaded to sell shares in companies with South African operations. The European American Banking Corporation, a consortium of banks (including the Midland) which provided large loans in the mid seventies, has agreed to arrange no further loans for the South African government or its agencies. Barclays Bank sold its defence bonds (loans directly for defence), but said it would continue to lend to South Africa in other ways. The campaign has won support from the Labour and Liberal parties (but the Labour government did not implement Labour Party conference resolutions) and from a number of big unions. But use of the unions' industrial power against South Africa has been more difficult to arrange. In early 1977 the Union of Post Office Workers (UPW) decided to black all South African mail during the trade union week of action on apartheid, but the UPW was prevented from carrying out the blacking by court action initiated by the business-backed National Association for Freedom. In other European countries, unions were more successful during the week of action, e.g. dockers imposed complete bans on the handling of South African goods and ships. This type of union action can be effective in the short run, and is important as a demonstration of support for the campaign. But the campaign has so far failed to get the long-run blacking of South African goods.

The Anti-Apartheid Movement has also been unable significantly to shift the British government's policy. The government makes gestures but refuses to do things which make their gestures effective, e.g. the Labour government introduced its own arms embargo but repeatedly used its veto in the UN Security Council against making the UN voluntary arms embargo mandatory. Britain abstained on a UN resolution imposing an oil embargo on South Africa to prevent sanctions-busting in Rhodesia. The government has also refused to take powers to prevent British companies from undermining the arms embargo by helping to develop South Africa's domestic armaments industry. Although British Leyland, a company with major interests in South Africa, is now state-owned, the government refuses to make Leyland (South Africa) implement policies on, for example, recognition of black trade unions, which it has itself approved and urged on other companies.[13] In general, the government will not contemplate economic disengagement from South Africa. There is no sign of the immediate investment and credit freeze

In a broadcast on Radio South Africa, the British ambassador to South Africa explains why the British Government has used its veto in the Security Council in favour of South Africa:
'. . . it is because we have so many interests in common with you . . ., because we have enormous investments in your country — the biggest investments of any country in South Africa, which we hope will remain profitable and remain sound, because we buy from you more than any other country and would like to go on doing this, even because we would like once again to play international cricket and international rugby with you . . .' (March 1977)
Source: quoted in *British Leyland in Britain and in South Africa*, Coventry Trades Council and Coventry Anti-Apartheid Movement.

demanded by the AAM. The government considers disengagement too damaging to British interests. It fears that disengagement would worsen Britain's existing balance of payments difficulties. In a letter to Jack Jones in 1976, the Prime Minister said: 'A trade ban would do great damage to employment and to our prospects for economic recovery.' The Western powers, more generally, have refused to take action against South Africa because it is seen as a bastion against communism in Africa and as strategically important.

To change its policy on this, the government would have to be convinced that public solidarity with black South Africans was strong enough to make people willing to accept economic problems resulting from disengagement from South Africa. Although support for the AAM has grown in recent years, probably spurred on by the Soweto killings (for example, between 1973 and 1976, the TUC became tougher in its opposition to British links with apartheid), the government has yet to be convinced that this public opinion exists. The possibilities for further action seem to be two-fold: *Either* activists continue, through the AAM and other organisations, the work of mobilising public opinion, making small gains on the way to the hoped for major disengagement. *Or* they may work for fundamental political change *in Britain itself* on the theory that it is unrealistic to expect a basically profit orientated system to disengage from a major profit earning area.

The same sort of argument can be applied to the baby foods case — you can't expect the companies to put humanitarian considerations before profit, since profit is their raison d'etre. *So perhaps the most effective thing people can do is to work towards some form of non-profit, non-exploitative system in the West — a system in which the companies will no longer exist.* The relevance to the Third World of political action on British issues is explored in the next chapter.

Notes and References

1. I shall only discuss voluntary groups in this context although the strategy is, of course, followed by the British Aid Programme. However most readers will be involved in the strategy through their support work for voluntary groups rather than through working for the government. See also the list of groups at the end of this book.
2. VSO — Voluntary Service Overseas, UNAIS — United Nations Association International Service, CIIR — Catholic Institute for International Relations, and IVS — International Voluntary Service.
3. Quotes from War on Want, *Choices for Change*.
4. *War on Want Yearly Report 1976—7.*
5. J. Briscoe, 'Improving Health Care where health is underdeveloped: do voluntary agencies (particularly Oxfam) help in Bangladesh?' unpublished paper commissioned by Oxfam, Dacca, 1978.
6. Briscoe, *op.cit.*, p. 7.
7. Jørgen Lissner, *The Politics of Altruism: the political behaviour of*

voluntary development agencies, (Lutheran World Federation, 1977).

8. The British Volunteer Programme is the structure which groups the four Government supported volunteer sending agencies (VSO, IVS, UNAIS and CIIR) together with Returned Volunteer Action (RVA), the British Council and the Ministry of Overseas Development.

9. *The British Volunteer Programme: An Evaluation*, (Overseas Development Group, University of East Anglia, 1978).

10. See 'The Baby Food Controversy: Three Years Later', *Ideas and Action* No. 117, 1977, (FAO, Rome).

11. See S. Clarke, 'Changing Patterns of International Investment in South Africa and the Disinvestment Campaign', (Anti-Apartheid Movement, 1978).

12. Information in this section is based on reports in *Anti-Apartheid News*, 1977 and 1978, the newspaper of the Anti-Apartheid Movement.

13. 'British Leyland in Britain and South Africa', Coventry Trades Council and Coventry Anti-Apartheid Movement, 1977.

4. Strategies for Change II: Political Action in Britain

I suggested at the end of the last chapter that political action in Britain on domestic British issues may be just as relevant to the Third World as more obviously Third World orientated 'development action'. This domestic political action may seem unappealing to those whose main concern is the Third World. To many returned volunteers, for example, British problems — e.g. homelessness or unemployment — seem trivial compared to the absolute want they have seen in the Third World. Hence these returned volunteers won't have much sympathy with groups in Britain trying to agitate on these domestic problems. The struggles of, for example, trade unions and students may seem the petty and selfish actions of relatively rich people fighting for a bigger slice of the cake. The returned volunteer has seen that *everyone* in Britain is materially well-off compared to most of the world and is convinced that most people would have to accept a lower standard of living if world resources were more equally shared. Hence many returned volunteers become alienated from British society and politics on their return.

I think this attitude is short-sighted. Even granted the over-riding importance of Third World poverty, still the most effective thing one can do *may* be to work towards fundamental political change in Britain. Everyone is faced with a choice: *Either* work for limited changes (e.g. restrictions on the baby food companies), which are more likely to be attainable in the short run but which will have only a marginal effect on the living conditions of the Third World poor; *Or* work to change the whole basis of the system so that, for example, exploitative British companies no longer exist. The latter strategy would have a much larger effect on the Third World poor, but is of course much harder to achieve. There is no one 'right choice' in my opinion: it depends on both objective circumstances (e.g. the political situation in Britain at any time) and on the personal interests, knowledge and abilities of the individual making the choice.

Most of the radical groups that a returned volunteer would be likely to join are, I think, working for a *common*, fundamental change. They mostly share the revolutionary ideal of a much more equal distribution of power in society. It's a revolutionary ideal because it is so far from our present reality — in which most people are powerless. The radical groups vary much more on what changes are conceived to be necessary to achieve the sharing of power.

I believe, along with the left-wing groups, that *socialism in the sense of collective ownership of economic resources is a necessary condition of achieving a more equal distribution of power* — for, as was said in Chapter I, capitalism has an inherent dynamic tendency towards the concentration of control of economic resources and therefore towards the concentration of power. The trend is for Western economies to be controlled by fewer and fewer large companies: for example, in Britain in 1970 the top hundred manufacturing firms controlled nearly *half* of net manufacturing output; whereas in 1950 they controlled only a fifth and in 1910 only 15%.[1] These

Percentage of Net Manufacturing Output Controlled by the 100 largest Firms in Britain

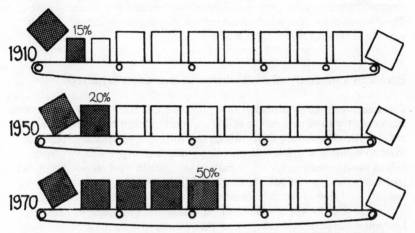

S. Prais, *The Evolution of Giant Firms,* (Oxford Economic Papers, 1974).

firms are themselves controlled by a tiny class of managers. Personal wealth is also highly concentrated. In Britain, again, latest estimates from the Royal Commission on the Distribution of Income and Wealth[2] show that the richest 1% owns over 25% of personal wealth; the richest 5% owns over 50%.

But collective ownership of economic resources is not a *sufficient* condition for a more equal distribution of power: the example of the USSR shows that it is not enough in itself, since private firms can be replaced by state firms without changing their authoritarian structure. As well as collective ownership, we need new democratic structures at work and in the community to give ordinary people real control over their own lives.

I believe that if this democratic form of socialism were established in the West, it would be of enormous benefit to the Third World: because it would mean the beginning of an end both to the exploitation of the Third World by the West, and to Western support for oppressive Third World power elites — thereby giving the Third World poor majority a much greater chance of taking control of *their* lives. Again, state ownership by itself isn't enough to bring about an end to exploitation of the Third World by the West. The USSR, some would argue, has exploited Eastern Europe, for example. But I think a truly *democratic* socialist system would end exploitation because it would depend on the creation of new values incompatible with exploitation. Such a system could not survive unless our present materialist, individualist ethic were replaced by values which stress responsibility to the community, global as well as national. The transition towards these new values would, of course, be tremendously difficult but, unless this re-education is accomplished, any democratic socialist revolution will degenerate back into hierarchy and authoritarianism.

To sum up: a more equal distribution of power, the common goal of so much radical activity, means a democratic form of socialism in my view, and its establishment in the West would be of fundamental importance to the Third World poor. Hence it is an aim worth working for in Britain, even if your main concern is the Third World.

How can a more equal distribution of power be achieved?

This question is *the* basic revolutionary problem and there are no easy answers. I can only try to describe some of the approaches taken by different radical groups. The radicals vary from Labour left wing to revolutionary socialists, from community activists to supporters of the 'alternative society', from radical professionals (teachers, social workers, health workers, etc.) to industrial militants, from socialist feminists to black liberationists. But their answers start from a common basic element: they all recognise the need to loosen the grip on people's minds of the ruling ideology, since this ideology legitimises the current system. To achieve change, people must be convinced that the system is against their interests and that alternatives are possible, that collectively people have the power to make changes. 'Loosening the grip of the ruling ideology' means exposing the conventional wisdom's mystifications and falsehoods, showing people that society *isn't* what the ideology says it is.

What is this conventional wisdom? I would describe it as follows: The modern British system deserves our support because, although it's not perfect, essentially it works for 'the greatest good of the greatest number'. Firstly, free enterprise (suitably controlled) creates *affluence* – look at the average standard of living today compared with forty years ago. This affluence has, of course, to be paid for by work, and work is undeniably unpleasant for many people. But one of the great strengths of the free enterprise system is its ability to generate technical progress, which gradually reduces the necessary hours of work, thus increasing leisure time in which to enjoy affluence. (The left-of-centre addition to this argument is that the system can be controlled by government so as to make sure that the benefits of technical progress are equally shared – free enterprise left to itself would just use technical progress to put people out of jobs.) Secondly, the system is *democratic* and *liberal*, so everyone has a share in political power, whatever their social position. Everyone has the right to express their views and to join the political party of their choice. Hence the system is capable of reform as and when people want it: it can be made to do what people want. Thirdly, the system gives reasonable *equality of opportunity* (again the left-of-centre adds the qualification — 'or can be made to give it') for everyone to develop her/his talents and provides a safety net (in the form of the Welfare State) for the unfortunate. It does this without stifling individual initiative and enterprise, and without removing incentives to work. With suitable safeguards, individual competition — 'striving for excellence' — brings benefits to the whole of society, not just to the successful individuals.

This is the conventional wisdom in the sense that it's the message about society that people continually receive. In my opinion, indoctrination ('mind control') is not too strong a word for it, despite our rights of free speech, the independent press and so on.

Spreading the conventional wisdom

For indoctrination to occur, it's not necessary to prohibit all opposition, or that the state should have monopolistic control of the media and other institutions. It's only necessary that the 'ideological competition should be so unequal as to give a crushing advantage to one side against the other.'[3] It seems to me only too evident that 'one side' — the conservative side — *does* have a crushing advantage in this ideological competition, even though dissent is tolerated and sometimes even expressed.

Trade Unions and The Media

Glasgow Dustmen's Strike: TV news reports concentrated on the health hazard of uncollected rubbish, at the expense of the causes of the strike:

13 week period during 1975	BBC1	BBC2	ITN
No. of reports	40	19	43
No. of reports mentioning cause of strike	11	6	19

British Leyland's Engine Tuners' Strike, 1975: The Prime Minister referred to the 'manifestly avoidable stoppages' caused by *both* management *and* labour. In 29 later references to the PM's speech on news bulletins, only the work-force was cited as responsible for stoppages.

No. of references to British Leyland's	BBC1	BBC2	ITN
'strike problems'	22	8	33
'management failings'	5	3	8
'company investment policy'	1	2	0

Source: Glasgow University Media Research Group, quoted in Beharrell and Philo, *Trade Unions and the Media*, (Macmillan, 1977).

Take the media: most mass circulation newspapers are hostile even to Labour, let alone to more radical parties and ideas. The activities of unions are continually presented as being against the 'national interest'. Workers are portrayed as pursuing narrow, selfish class interests when they go on strike, whereas the behaviour of businessmen is rarely described in class terms.[4] Radio and TV are officially impartial, but this impartiality is defined in narrow party political terms. The BBC may not be biased as between Labour, Liberal or Conservative, but this impartiality stops at the point where the political consensus itself stops.[5] More radical views are seldom allowed.

Media Support for the Tories

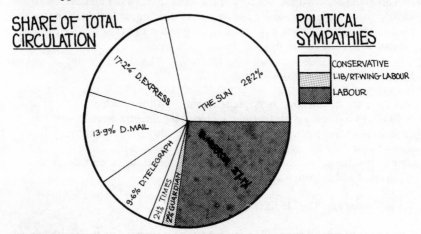

"The Press and the Next Election", *Labour Research,* January 1979. Circulation figures based on Audit Bureau of Circulation statistics, Jan-June 1978.

Advertising is another important part of the media. Generally, advertising is 'selling' a lot more than a particular product: in our type of economic system, one of the characteristics of advertising 'is the intention to manipulate people into buying a "way of life" as well as goods.'[6] Advertising seeks to gain support for free enterprise, by suggesting that business is virtuous and responsible, obsessed with *your* welfare rather than profit; profit is of course necessary, but primarily so that the corporation can continue to serve *you* the customer. Advertising tries to associate socially approved values (reliability, security, integrity, parental care) both with particular products and with business generally. Equally important, it fosters the belief that the only route to fulfilment, happiness and success is through private acquisitiveness, mainly in the context of family life.

Mass entertainment — films, popular fiction, TV — also purveys an ideological message. As with advertising, the message is overwhelmingly in favour of the status quo. Mass entertainment exalts the nation, the family, free enterprise, individualism, law and order, anti-communism (think of all the spy thrillers you've read/seen). There is almost nothing from the other side: there are no revolutionary equivalents of James Bond, for example.

The media is only one element of the indoctrination apparatus. The educational system is equally important. Schools and universities probably do generally avoid overt party bias, and are politically neutral in that sense. But in a broader sense of politics, they are anything but neutral. They inculcate acceptance of our type of capitalism as fundamentally worthy of support and they instil other feelings and values — competitiveness, individualism, a sense of personal inadequacy in those who fail — which are more likely to maintain the system than disrupt it.

Political parties are also powerful propagandists for the system. The Conservative Party is obviously an important disseminator of pro-capitalist, anti-socialist ideas, but the Labour Party may be equally important in gaining support for the system. Although the Labour Party may disagree on details, it does not question the fundamental soundness of regulated capitalism. The conventional wisdom described above is broadly accepted by *both* major parties; it forms the premises, often implicit, on which most political argument is based.

The radicals, on the other hand, question much if not all of this conventional wisdom. Different groups concentrate on attacking different parts of the ideology. A multi-pronged attack is necessary because you can't reach everyone in the same way. People's experiences of the system differ. A returned volunteer, for example, may come to believe that fundamental change in the system is necessary because s/he has seen its oppressive effects in the Third World, whereas a factory worker has felt its oppression for him or herself, as part of everyday work experience. But though a diverse approach is necessary to reach a wider spectrum of people, it has its costs in disunity. As mentioned above, I believe that many radical groups are fighting for essentially the same goals. But unless they realise this and create some overall structure which reflects it, much of their energy will be dissipated.

At the risk of some distortion, we can distinguish two main types of strategy used by radical groups to loosen the grip of the ruling ideology. They are (1) *the creation of alternative structures* (e.g. communes, co-operatives, free schools, community arts centres, women's centres). The aim is to create something as much outside present structures as possible, to demonstrate that other ways of organising economic and social life are feasible; (2) *working within existing structures but campaigning to change them* — either at work, or in the local community, or nationally.

Radical strategies I: The creation of alternative structures

This strategy is particularly characteristic of (a) the ecologists (this name will probably offend some people but I can't think of a better one) — i.e. those people who strongly reject the materialism and associated environmental irresponsibility of our society; and (b) libertarian socialists – people who are suspicious of authoritarian tendencies in the traditional left. There is, of course, some overlapping. Libertarians and ecologists are also campaigners, while the traditional left may also set up co-operatives – though on the whole the traditional left dismisses the 'creation of alternative structures' as irrelevant to the main struggle.

> 'In 1941, it seemed likely that US production would double in about twenty years; thus a working week of about twenty hours could replace the then 40.6 hours. How would men employ their greatly increased leisure? The question never arose. It turned out that production indeed effectively doubled, and in less time than predicted, but in 1965 the working week had actually increased to 41.1 hours.
>
> What was being produced in that 'unnecessary' twenty hours a week? Some real additions to comfort and well-being of course, . . . but it is evident that the bulk of the time cannot be accounted for in this way: to see what it produced, we must look at the chrome on household appliances, the aluminium beer can, the wider acceptance of a 'planned obsolescence' in automobiles unrelated to their basic performance, a multitude of new 'created' needs such as men's toilet aids, plastic packaging, detergents instead of soap . . . Is the sum total of such pleasures, marginal at best, worth twenty hours a week of compulsory labour for life?'
>
> (Alan Roberts, 'Consumerism and the Ecological Crisis', SERA.)

The ecologists and libertarians believe that the affluence lauded by the conventional wisdom is largely a myth: this kind of affluence is only possible at the expense of the destruction of the environment, so in the long run industrialised consumer society may not even be sustainable. They wouldn't see it as desirable either: they reject our society's conception of the 'good life' as the unending accumulation of consumer goods. They also question conventional wisdom's assumption that work is more or less bound to be unpleasant and that, therefore, we should look to technical progress to reduce the necessity for work as much as possible. Instead, they think of work – productive activity – as an essential part of human life. Work only becomes degrading and unpleasant when it is non-autonomous, when people are forced to work but have no control over how the work should be organised because control is vested in a small minority (private capitalists or a state bureaucracy) who pursue their own aims – profit, military power, etc. For example, in the West it is the pursuit of profit not technological imperatives, which leads to the endless division of labour and mechanisation of work, so that work for many people means performing one or two simple operations, eight hours a day, five days a week, year after year. The point is, technology doesn't *have* to be used in that way.

From this rejection of consumerism has developed a vision of an 'alternative society' consisting of small decentralised communities, economically self-sufficient, environmentally stable and democratically organised. Material consumption will be replaced, as the main source of satisfaction, by participation in creative, non-mechanised work, by having a real measure of control over one's work and community, by living in harmony with the environment rather than tearing it apart, by the better human relationships that will develop as people once more live in communities rather than in the present urban sprawl.

With this vision before them, a lot of people are trying to create the 'alternative society' here and now by their own individual action. This strategy is immediately satisfying for two reasons. Firstly, it allows people to demonstrate their criticism of society and commitment to the 'alternative' by dropping out of ordinary jobs. Since dropping out usually means living on a very low income, it allows people to show their rejection of consumerism in a vivid personal way. It unifies the personal and the political. Secondly, it's satisfying because it's creative — it allows people to experiment with new ways of living and working now rather than 'when the revolution comes'.

Both elements seem to me to be potentially important. I think it's important to have an ever-growing fund of experience of new ways of living, on which others can draw. After all, people need to be prepared for 'when the revolution comes' — otherwise there's a strong chance that any revolution will replace capitalist authoritarianism with socialist authoritarianism. Creating alternative projects can also be effective propaganda against the system *if* other people get to know about it. To be effective in either way, alternative projects must be part of a wider political campaign or movement; otherwise, the criticism of them as a 'cop out' seems justified: for how can the change in lifestyle of a small minority bring about the alternative society?

Uhuru

An alternative project which seems to have integrated 'lifestyle' and more conventional politics is Uhuru in Oxford. Uhuru consists of a wholefood shop and café, run by a collective of full-time workers and volunteers. They try to organise democratically and to break down the normal division of labour: e.g. everyone takes a turn at the business side of the project (ordering, pricing, and coping with the accounts). It participates in community projects (e.g. a community newspaper, a welfare rights advice centre, helping the homeless, helping on playschemes, a consumer food co-operative), and in Third World campaigns (e.g. selling co-operatively grown Tanzanian coffee as part of a campaign to explain the exploitative nature of present world trading arrangements).

The political outlook behind this is very well explained in *Uhuru – A Working Alternative* – the collective's description of the project.[7] They are critical of traditional left vanguard parties but are –

> uncertain about a real alternative road to political power . . . We want to see everyone grow in confidence and political understanding to the extent that, if a crisis situation ever arises, when social structures are amenable to being overturned and rebuilt, then the people will be able to force the 'vanguard' to obey them; and, if crisis does not arise, that people will nonetheless be able to make progress in democratising their industries, institutions and families. To that end we back . . . the whole range of community and industry based struggle, organisation and self-help, in so far as it does increase both awareness of the power that can be taken and commitment to the values of equality, co-operation, love and the solidarity of the alienated and the oppressed.'
>
> And Uhuru's role in this libertarian struggle for people's power? We can be useful as a meeting place . . . for all the left groups. We tend through our open image to involve people who would not go near a political party, but who gradually become politicised through Uhuru . . . We do have 5 to 6 people with half their week free for community/political activity . . . In the long term there is much to be said for spreading . . . a diet that does not waste the earth's resources . . . (But) it is not our main aim to change people's diets or to conserve energy. We aim to be an unconventional form of politicisation and are learning through experience. (pages 23–4)

Impact of the alternative society on the Third World

Suppose the dream came true and something like the alternative society was set up in the West: how would it affect the Third World? Some have argued that the alternative society will hinder development in the Third World. The pursuit of economic self-sufficiency will cut off markets for Third World exports. The anti-pollution, anti-agribusiness stance of the ecology movement is often regarded as a rich country luxury, or even as a disguised method of preventing the Third World from industrialising. Surely, it is said, countries facing starvation cannot afford *not* to use pesticides, inorganic fertilisers etc. Can protection of the environment take precedence over food supply?

If the development of the Third World rests solely on foreign trade and on Western-type technology, then the alternative society could indeed prevent the Third World from ever catching up. But I've tried to argue that the most basic cause of under-development is present-day political and economic structures – exploitative trade and technological backwardness are symptoms of these. The alternative society would, I think, help true development in the Third World, because it is very unlikely that the small, self-sufficient, alternative communities could engage in large-scale exploitation of the Third World, either by trade or through direct investment. Military interference becomes correspondingly less likely. I think these benefits would more than outweigh the costs to the Third World associated with disruption of export markets. In the long run, this could help promote self-reliant development in the Third World.

Radical Strategies II: Working within the system, but campaigning to change it

(a) At Work

One of the most important ways of reaching people is through their work experience, since it is at work that conventional wisdom's talk of freedom and power-sharing in our society can most obviously be seen to be a myth. Probably most people feel almost completely powerless at work. Work represents almost constant coercion and discipline, even for those in middle-class jobs (though the sanctions against 'disobedience' are more subtle in this case). Very few have the opportunity to plan what they should do, or when and how they should do it. People are 'free' to choose the jobs that suit them, but once in a job they have to accept the job description laid down by higher authority. And 'freedom to choose' is itself very limited for most people, especially for those without qualifications and especially in a time of high unemployment. All workers, as *individuals*, are in a very weak position to negotiate with employers on anything that affects their working lives. An individual worker has no bargaining power. S/he has to work to live, but has to compete with millions of others in the same position — so if s/he makes 'unreasonable' demands, the employer always has plenty of other workers to choose from.

The historic reaction to this powerlessness has been trade unionism: the only way to reduce the power disparity between the two sides is for workers to act as one and hence reduce the competition between them. There is little doubt that without the organised strength of the labour movement — the industrial power of the unions and the political power of the Labour Party — we would not be living under 'reformed capitalism', with reduced exploitation, improved working conditions, the Welfare State safety net, and some degree of employment protection. The labour movement's success has led to a continual cry from most of the media and from the Conservatives that 'the unions have too much power'. But how far does this power go? Trade unions can up to a point defend their members' interests, but their influence over vital management decisions on such matters as redundancy and the location of new investment is still limited. The development of multinational firms reduces bargaining power further: if workers are 'bolshie', firms can always build their plants somewhere else. *Fundamentally, trade unions have not challenged the power and right of management to make all the important decisions. They haven't produced a democratisation of work.* On the whole, trade unions haven't seen it as their function to fight for this. They have restricted their demands to those which can be met without a basic restructuring of firms. The unions have remained within the capitalist system, indeed have become increasingly integrated into it as successive governments have

63

involved them in 'making the system work better' through the 'social contract', the industrial strategy, etc.

Does the official trade union movement help to 'loosen the grip of the ruling ideology?' Yes and no, but mostly no. Yes, because the unions give industrial workers some sense of their power to change things. No, because by becoming an integral part of capitalism they have made capitalism appear more acceptable, more legitimate. It is easy for apologists for the system to make it appear that workers are now equally represented in the system with capitalists, that the old exploitative kind of capitalism has gone for good.

But to anyone interested in changing society, the unions are crucially important, despite the conservatism of much of the trade union hierarchy — because no other remotely radical group has the power, actual and potential, of organised labour. (As was shown in Chapter 3, campaigning groups like the Anti-Apartheid Movement are well aware of this, and try to get the unions to join their campaigns.) And if the labour movement can't be radicalised, there's not much hope of radicalising the rest of society — since the unions' criticisms of capitalism, though not always reflected in action, make them closer to the radical approach than most other groups in society. So what do you do — join a union and try to change it from the inside, or give this up as hopeless and look for others who are interested in creating new, radical worker organisations? As usual there's no general answer, and both types of strategy are being followed at the moment.

Unofficial unionism: In response to the increasing moderation of trade union leaderships, workers have been forced to develop new forms of organisation to represent them. Throughout the post-war period, but particularly since the sixties, rank and file militancy has been expressed through informal organisations (typically shop stewards committees) which cut across official trade union structures.

The growth of shop floor organisation has been greeted with intense hostility by the media and the establishment in general. The reason for this is clear. Through official trade unionism, conflict between labour and capital has become institutionalised: it can take place without fundamentally threatening the capitalist system. Shop floor organisation, on the other hand, is seen as a threat to this institutionalisation of conflict and hence to the power of capital. Thus both Labour and Conservative governments have attempted to control what they see as the 'anarchy' of the shop floor.[8]

In many cases this 'anarchy' represents the attempts by workers to win some measure of control over their working environment. Although official trade unionism may have conceded to management the right to decide work methods and organisation, rank and file workers are engaged in a continual battle with management for 'job control'. Thus a high proportion of unofficial strikes are generated by disputes over matters such as the speed of assembly lines, manning levels on each line and the allocation of work. In factories where shop floor organisation is strong, and when market conditions are favourable (so that the company is more vulnerable to the interruption of production), workers have been able to challenge managerial autonomy.[9]

Clearly, to the power holders in our society, 'anarchy' results when the powerless gain a little bit of power over their working lives. To the power holders, unofficial strikers are irresponsible 'wreckers', selfishly disrupting industry on which 'the nation' depends. I see it very differently. To me, these workers are fighting against the dehumanising practice of 'scientific management' which, in the interests of productivity, attempts to reduce the worker to an unthinking appendage of the machine on which s/he is working. The basic principle of scientific management is, in the words of its founder Frederick Taylor, that 'the workman is told minutely just what he is to do and how he is to do it and that any improvement he makes upon the orders given to him is fatal to success.' In my view, no human being ought to submit to such a negation of her or his creativity and autonomy. People should not be appendages — and that's what many shop floor workers are saying, implicitly or explicitly, when they walk out or sabotage the production line.

'I have not been able to discover that repetitive labour injures a man in any way.' (Henry Ford I)

For maximum efficiency, it is necessary that the worker 'shall be so stupid and phlegmatic that he more nearly resembles in his mental make-up an ox than any other type.' (Frederick Taylor, *Principles of Scientific Management*)

But does industrial technology have to be like that? 'Every machine that helps every individual has a place, but there should be no place for machines that concentrate power in a few hands and turn the masses into mere machine minders, if indeed they do not make them unemployed.' (Gandhi)

'We must do away with machines that appear to treat men as mere appendages, and replace them with machines that the individual can operate in a way that is both socially productive and personally fulfilling.' (D. Dickson, *Alternative Technology and the Politics of Technical Change*, Fontana)

The right to socially useful work: Until recently most shop floor action has been defensive and limited. Workers have attacked their own employers, often without seeing that the real enemy is the capitalist system of production, of which 'scientific management' is a necessary part. The last few years, however, have seen a growing rank and file campaign which *is* based on a critique of the whole system. This is the campaign for the 'right to socially useful work', pioneered by the Lucas Aerospace Combine Shop Stewards

Committee and since joined by other workers in the military sector, in power engineering and the building industry.

The Lucas workers realised that their jobs were at risk, both because of possible cuts in military spending (Lucas Aerospace makes military equipment) and because of corporate rationalisation plans. In the last six years, the work force has been reduced from 18,000 to 11,300, and the company plans a further reduction to 10,000. The Lucas workers did not want to call for more military spending in order to protect their jobs. Hence they devised an 'Alternative Corporate Plan': a detailed technical description of 150 socially useful products which the skilled workers at Lucas could make. The list includes energy-saving products such as a hybrid diesel-electric car, solar collectors and windmills, and medical products such as kidney machines and artificial limb control units.

The philosophy behind the Plan explicitly rejects the established priorities of our society: 'There is something seriously wrong with a society which can produce a level of technology to design and build a Concorde, but cannot produce enough simple urban heating systems to protect the old age pensioners who are dying each winter of hypothermia.'[10] The Plan also rejects the de-humanising technology currently used in industry. It 'sought to find . . . those forms of technology which would give full vent to the creativity of the hands and minds of the workers, and that could be produced by non-hierarchical forms of industrial organisations.'[11]

The Lucas workers realise that they cannot change society on their own:

> Progress can only be minimal so long as our society is based on the assumption that profits come first and people come last. Thus the question is a political one, whether we like it or not. Perhaps the most significant feature of the Corporate Plan is that we trade unionists are attempting to transcend the narrow economism which has characterised trade union activity in the past, and are extending our demands to the extent of questioning the products on which we work and the way in which we work on them.

The company has responded predictably. It has rejected the Plan as commercially unviable, and has rejected the right of workers to influence corporate policy. Management has refused even to meet the Combine Committee in the three years since the Plan was published, on the grounds that the Committee is undemocratic and unconstitutional because it is outside the official collective bargaining structure. For the same reason, the trade union leadership has also been unenthusiastic about the Plan. Hence so far none of the Plan proposals has been implemented.

Moreover, in March 1978, the company announced a reorganisation which would involve the closure of several plants and the loss of at least 1,400 more jobs. The Combine Committee has promised active resistance to the closures. Detailed plans are being worked out to determine which products in the

Corporate Plan could be produced at the threatened sites. Attempts to close these plants will be met by demands that the workers should be allowed to work on these alternative products, backed up by the occupation of factories if necessary.[12] *For, as the Lucas workers say, why should skilled workers be thrown on the dole, when for no extra cost to the country they could be paid to make things which (like kidney machines) people desperately need?*

Radical professionals: Perhaps of more relevance to returned volunteers is the growth of groups pressing for a radical practice within their occupation/ profession. These groups are also concerned with the *content* of work rather than pay and conditions. Radicals with middle-class jobs face a 'within versus without' problem, and it's often acutely felt by returned volunteers: 'Should I work within the system, because we shouldn't allow the system to be operated entirely by the right wing? – I might be able to push things in a radical direction. Or is it impossible for me to have any effect, so I'm just wasting my time and might as well drop out?' The answer depends on a host of factors: which part of the system you're working in (there may be more scope in teaching than in the civil service, for example), what other oppor- tunities are available and, of course, on your own personality.

But for those who decide to stay in the system, radical professional groups are essential.[13] They can make the strategy of changing things from the inside a feasible one, which it generally isn't at the level of individual action. An individual who tries to question orthodoxy within her/his institution is almost bound to come into conflict with her/his bosses and may be disci- plined. An essential defence against this is collective action with others of similar views.

A radical movement seems to be spreading in education, an area of particular importance to returned volunteers. The movement is expressed in journals like *Radical Education, Hard Cheese, Libertarian Education.*[14] Though teachers have no industrial power to speak of, they are important in the battle of ideas. The education system is one of the main ideological trans- mission belts in society. Hence radical teachers, *if* they can convince enough of their colleagues and the public, are potentially in a good position to 'loosen the grip of the ruling ideology'.

Radical teachers have influenced public opinion. They have helped make people aware of the myth of equality of opportunity. It's now well known that working-class children have far fewer chances than their middle-class peers: the schools they attend have fewer resources; the homes they come from have fewer books, papers, opportunities for adult conversation, dis- cussion of ideas; their ways of speech, interests, habits are too often rejected by their middle-class teachers. As the diagram shows, the children of 'profes- sional and technical' fathers were still, in the early 1970's, *nine* times more likely than those from manual homes to enter a university. The disadvantages are particularly severe in the case of black or brown kids. In Inner London, for example, immigrants are 17% of the school population, but 34% of the 'educationally subnormal' school population.[15]

Is more money – positive discrimination in favour of the educationally

Class and Higher Education

PERCENTAGE OF CHILDREN OBTAINING A UNIVERSITY EDUCATION

	Mid-1950s	Early-1970s	1970s Non-Manual Backgrounds	
ALL BACKGROUNDS	‖‖ 4%	‖‖‖‖‖ 9%	PROFESSIONAL & TECHNICAL ‖‖‖‖‖‖‖‖‖‖‖‖‖‖‖‖‖‖	35%
NON-MANUAL BACKGROUNDS	‖‖‖‖‖‖‖ 10%	‖‖‖‖‖‖‖‖‖‖‖‖ 18%	ADMINISTRATIVE & MANAGERIAL ‖‖‖‖‖‖‖‖‖‖‖	21%
MANUAL BACKGROUNDS	‖ 1½%	‖‖‖ 4%	OTHER NON-MANUAL ‖‖‖‖‖‖‖	10½%

Adapted from Westergaard and Riesler, *Class in Capitalist Society,* (Penguin, 1975), p.322.

disadvantaged — the answer? Radicals would say that, though more money would help, our school system will never produce equality because that's not what it's designed for. The *real* function of schooling is quite different from the appearance. It is *not*, primarily, about learning. It *is* about grading, about selecting people to fill slots in a highly unequal, hierarchical society and instilling habits of submission to that hierarchy. Schools put everyone into a contest that only a few can win, but teach that failure is due not to the unfair nature of the contest, but to the fault of the individual. It is in schools that 'the mass of our citizens in all classes learn that life is inevitably routine, depersonalized, venally graded; that it is best to toe the mark and shut up; that there is no place for spontaneity, open sexuality, free spirit.'[16]

> **Schooling and inequality**
> '. . . the hierarchical organization of schools, and the process of competitive selection to which the children are subjected, may well serve to familiarize pupils with the logic of inequality that pervades the society at large; to reduce potential opposition to that inequality through such early familiarity; and to make many or most children breathe a sigh of relief when they are released from school, into subordinate positions in adult life, after long experience of educational rejection. Such indirect support from the school system for the established order may be much more important than direct indoctrination . . .'
> J. Westergaard and H. Resler, *Class in a Capitalist Society*, (Penguin)

What can libertarian teachers do about all this, assuming they don't drop out and start a free school? Putting libertarian ideas into practice in the classroom is incredibly difficult, since the libertarian classroom will inevitably be used as an outlet for the frustrations and tensions that build up in 'normal' (i.e. repressive) classrooms. The kids will riot and the teacher will be ticked off by the head. Here, of course, the support of radical colleagues is vital. The alternative education press reports on some brave souls who are trying.

Radical teachers have also investigated educational materials, exposing the racist, sexist and class biases that are so prevalent in them. Some of this work has begun to take effect: for example, official bodies such as the Schools Council now recognise the existence of racist bias in educational materials. Apart from its intrinsic importance to our own society, the elimination of racism is also important for the Third World, since much hostility to the Third World is linked to racial prejudice.

(b) In the Community
The community action movement is a clear example of a reaction to powerlessness. People are told they live in a power sharing democracy, but find that all the important decisions — on housing, roads, schools, hospitals, employment — are made for them without their participation. Community activists show that our much praised democracy is something of a sham. It doesn't give people the right to control decisions; it's limited to the right to choose, and that only once every few years, *who* should make the decisions *for* you. After voting, people are expected to abdicate responsibility to professional politicians and the state bureaucracy. Community groups refuse to abdicate. As the people most concerned about what happens in their communities, they have demanded the right to participate, to influence, to control.

Community action has also attacked the myth of affluence. The movement has been especially strong in poor areas, areas which have *not* shared in the general improvement in the standard of living. Activists have shown that 'enlightened capitalism' has not solved the problem of poverty. There are still many communities with poor housing, high unemployment, inadequate social services. (For example, in parts of Bradford, the infant mortality rate is higher than in Jamaica.) They have tried to communicate their sense of outrage that this should exist in the midst of overall affluence.

What do community activists do? A few examples: —
—They start community newspapers. Since so much of the local press is highly conservative, people have tried to start alternative papers to publicise a radical view of what's happening in their communities. They are very often organs of protest about, for example, proposed redevelopments, council housing, lack of community facilities (from playspace to hospitals to community centres).
—They protest about their housing conditions. For example, a group of council tenants at Sporle Court, high rise flats in Wandsworth, complained of repairs not done, of damp, of lifts not working and more generally of the problems of high rise living. They produced a report, 'Sporle Court — an everyday story

of housing mismanagement', which was given lots of press publicity and galvanised council officers into action. They arranged a meeting with the tenants. Within a week of the meeting, most of the small repairs had been done. The bigger problems were still to be solved — but it became Wandsworth Council's policy to move families out of high rise flats as soon as other housing becomes available.[17]

—They try to protect their communities. An example of this is the long-running campaign which has come to be known as the 'Battle for Tolmers Square', in North London.[18] The Tolmers area is mixed — residential, shops and small businesses. Since the mid fifties, the area has been threatened with comprehensive redevelopment. Because of its position close to Central London, the area has attracted property developers as a lucrative site for new offices.

In the late fifties and sixties the Tolmers Square Tenants Association successfully beat off the property developers. They didn't see why their community should be destroyed just so that another office block could (probably) stand empty in the Euston area. Because of their pressure, the local authorities refused planning permission for various office development schemes. One property developer, Stock Conversion, secretly bought up houses in the area, at prices far below their potential value, and so gained control of most of the land in the Tolmers area. The houses were allowed to fall into total disrepair to encourage the tenants to leave. Houses which became vacant were boarded up and left empty. Thus the area gradually decayed. Having got control of the land, Stock Conversion offered a deal to the Council: basically, if the Council allowed it to build offices, it would sell housing land to the Council at a much reduced price. A campaign was organised to stop the deal, mobilising a large number of groups including the residents' Tolmers Village Association and local Labour Party branches. The campaign got a lot of press and TV coverage and finally succeeded. The deal was called off.

The Tolmers Village Association (TVA) was determined to fight the destruction of the community. If they couldn't persuade the Council to take action, they did it themselves. They encouraged squatters to take over the empty houses, since this was the only way of preventing them from deteriorating. The influx of squatters went a long way towards re-creating the community. The TVA occupied a piece of vacant land and turned it into a community garden. Up to then, there had been nowhere for kids to play or for old people to sit, no trees, no gardens and nowhere to hold community events. They provided an advice service for the residents, and organised social and cultural events to help foster community feeling. And the TVA kept up a constant effort to publicise the area's problems and to pressurise the Council into protecting the community by buying the land itself. In 1975 the Council did buy the land, but the battle was not over. Because the land was so expensive, the Council maintained that offices would have to be built to help finance any scheme. But, by that time, the TVA had more or less collapsed. It had flourished for two years, but like many

community action groups found it difficult to maintain momentum.
The strategy of community action: The strategy of community action groups
so far seems to be to seize power where they can, to challenge the power
structure on particular local issues. The limitations of this are obvious: the
really big problems, like unemployment and poverty, can't be solved at local
level.[19] They need a national re-allocation of resources, but this is outside
the control of local power holders. Without such a re-allocation, successful
community action may only shift problems from one community to a less

well-organised one: e.g. in a time of general public expenditure cuts, a success-ful fight to keep a hospital open will only be at the expense of health services in another community where protest hasn't developed.

To overcome these limitations, there needs to be a community politics movement: a coalition of community action groups which will provide con-tinuity, resources and a clear political direction. The idea is to base the challenge to the national power structure on the community as well as on the work place. Community activists say that the strategy for fundamental change can no longer be based solely on activating the industrial working class, because this class no longer exists in the old Marxist sense. The increased standard of living, expansion of white collar jobs, and the decline of tradi-tional working-class communities has led to the fragmentation of the working class, so that it can no longer be thought of as a homogeneous group whose interests are inevitably opposed to capitalism. This doesn't mean that indus-trial struggles are no longer important, but it does mean that they must be supplemented by struggles in a new setting: the community.

How could such a community based politics actually work? Presumably it would be a mixture of direct action on immediate local issues, forging a national alliance of community groups, linking up with industrial activists, plus attempts to win parliamentary/local elections. How far community politics should rely on traditional parliamentary methods for achieving change is an extremely difficult question. One danger is that electoral success will be made the excuse for sacrificing the practice of real participatory democracy. It is all too easy for elected politicians to adopt a paternalistic attitude towards the people who elected them. But as community action has grown out of disillusion with traditional electoral politics, possibly this danger may be avoided — or electoral politics will be boycotted altogether.

(c) The national political scene

Even if community and industrial struggles were more united, they can't, by themselves, achieve fundamental change in society. A more equal distri-bution of power requires action at the level of the state. Obviously, capitalist property relations can't be abolished without taking state power — and, as I argued earlier, the end of capitalism is an essential pre-requisite for a more equal distribution of power. What strategies do radicals have for taking state power? I think a lot of people, who are radical in the sense of recognising the need for a very different sort of society, are unwilling to think about this question. Radical change may seem so far in the future that they feel it is unnecessary to elaborate strategies for getting there — they'd prefer to con-tinue with the work of 'consciousness raising' in industrial, community and other struggles (i.e. the women's movement, and anti-racist, anti-fascist campaigns). But, on the other hand, there is no shortage of groups — from the Labour Party leftwards — which do have a worked out strategy. The basic division is between those who follow an electoral strategy and those who argue that fundamental change requires a revolution.
Electoral strategy: This has been the traditional strategy of the Labour Party.

Labour has assumed, reflecting the dominance of Fabianism within the party, that socialism can *gradually* be legislated into existence.[20] According to the Fabians, a socialist society could be produced by successive instalments of reform which would one day 'add up' to socialism. They assumed that this progression was inevitable once universal suffrage was achieved — all opponents would ultimately be powerless against it. The 1945 Labour government was Labour's chance to provide the first instalment of socialism. But, by 1948, Labour seemed to have sunk into inertia, and any remaining faith in the inevitability of progress was shattered by the election defeats of the fifties.

Why was Labour defeated? Basically, because Labour's 'socialist' reforms served to *regenerate* rather than overthrow the capitalist system. Thus industries were nationalised, but they became organised in such a way that they served private sector industry (by providing subsidised inputs) rather than the public. Moreover, nationalisation opened no new socialist perspectives: public sector workers remained just as powerless at work as their private sector counterparts. The Welfare State reforms were necessary and popular, but they too strengthened the system by making it seem fairer and therefore more acceptable to the subordinate classes.

The Labour leadership's response to the failure of Fabian strategy was essentially to abandon the socialist goal in favour of becoming the party of the mixed economy, 'enlightened capitalism'. Since the early sixties, Labour has presented itself as the party of efficiency, the party that can make capitalism 'work better'. We are always told to wait until economic problems are solved — *then* we can do something about poverty because then there'll be a 'bigger national cake to share out'. The Labour leaders talk more about 'incentives' than 'equality'.

Does this mean that nothing further can be hoped for from the Labour Party? Or is it possible to work within the party to change its policy? These questions will be considered later, but before going on to them, I'll try to describe a very different response to the failure of Fabian strategy.
Revolutionary strategy: Following Marx, revolutionary socialists would say that Fabian strategy could never have succeeded, because it was based on a fundamentally wrong analysis of the nature of the state in capitalist society.[21] The state, they say, is *not* a neutral arbiter between conflicting groups in society — though this is how conventional wisdom describes it. Rather, Marxists hold that the state is a set of institutions whose main purpose is to defend the predominance of the capitalist class. Democracy does not ensure the sharing of power between classes. The capitalist class rules *through* democratic state institutions, rather than by direct dictatorship as in earlier times (when the pre-industrial aristocracy virtually *was* the state).

Businessmen, though strongly represented in national and local government and in Parliament, are not the governing class as the aristocracy once was. But they do not need to be. As numerous studies have shown, the people at the top of all state institutions (the administration, nationalised industries, the judiciary, the military and the police, as well as the government

and Parliament) come overwhelmingly from the upper and middle classes, as do businessmen themselves.[22] A few people from working class backgrounds do enter the elite, and this may even be an increasing trend (though not, as the diagram opposite shows, as far as Parliament is concerned). But such people adopt the ideology of the elite and their high salaries enable them to become part of the property-owning classes.

Elites and Power in Britain: Higher Civil Servants

	Above Assistant Secretary in rank		The Upper Grades
	1939	1950	1967
Fathers were:			
Manual workers	9%	20%	17%
Semi or unskilled workers, manual workers	3%	3%	6%
Education:			
LEA School	16%	20%	35%
Oxbridge	66%	60%	51%

Source: R. Kelsall in Stanworth and Giddens (eds.) *Elites and Power in British Society*, (Cambridge University Press, 1974), p. 173.

As representatives of (or new entrants to) the privileged class, the state elites are likely to believe in and support the system that guarantees them their privilege. By background, values and/or interests, they are closely linked to the business world. On most occasions, they will believe that acting in the interests of business is also acting in the national interest. For example, the policies of the Labour government from 1974 to 1978 — the 'social contract', incomes policies, unemployment-creating cuts in public expenditure — were presented, probably sincerely, as essential for national recovery. But each of these policies strengthened the position of business vis à vis the working class.

%age of Labour MPs who were manual workers before entering Parliament

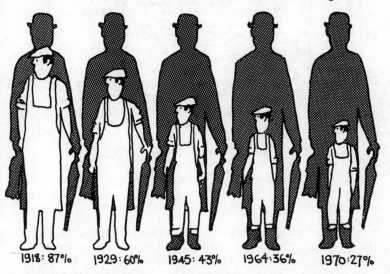

1918: 87%   1929: 60%   1945: 43%   1964: 36%   1970: 27%

W. Guttsman, in Stanworth and Giddens (eds.), *Elites and Power in British Society,* (Cambridge University Press, 1974), p.28.

I'm not trying to say that the ruling class is monolithic, or engaged in a conspiracy against the workers. Clearly there are sometimes divisions in the ruling class. Some government policies may favour one group of capitalists at the expense of another (e.g. nationalisation). But, on the whole, economic and state elites co-operate in maintaining our type of capitalist system.

Why has universal suffrage had so little effect on the distribution of power? Doesn't it show that most people are content with the system — because otherwise they could have voted it out? After all, Labour activists don't *have* to choose their leaders from the upper classes — they must do it because these leaders express views they support. This is true, but is only half the story because it ignores the indoctrination effort of the economically dominant classes (see pp. 57—59 above). Business owns most of the media (e.g. seven multinationals now control more than 90% of national newspaper sales);[23] business not the unions (let alone other radicals) has the resources to advertise; the property-owning classes dominate the 'Establishment' which controls the government, administration, political parties, education, the BBC, the churches. All this adds up to a formidable apparatus of ideological control, so that people are made to 'want' what the economically dominant classes want them to want.

Given these power relationships in the capitalist state and society, Marxists argue that it is impossible for 'the working class (to) take hold of the ready-made state apparatus and wield it for its own purposes' (Marx, *The Civil War in France*). In other words, capitalism won't let itself be legislated out of existence, and the Fabians were wrong to think that it ever could be. If the left wins an election, it has only won the *right* to change society, not the *power* to do it. The left may occupy the government, but the rest of the state and indoctrination apparatus is still controlled by the capitalist class. The Chilean experience shows what can happen to a government that tries to bring about fundamental economic and social change *within* the framework of the capitalist state.

Thus many have concluded that a revolution — socialising production and refashioning the state — is the only way. However, revolutionaries are divided on how the revolution is to be achieved. Some still stick to the Bolshevik model, in which the revolutionary party trains the vanguard of the working class, preparing for a seizure of power on the basis of a widespread popular uprising (as in Russia in 1917). This is not a coup d'état strategy, since the revolution can only succeed if a majority of the people want it. The task of the party is to raise the political consciousness of the working class so that the crises that, according to the theory, capitalism inevitably produces, can lead to uprising and revolution.

Raising consciousness involves supporting the working class on what may appear to be short-term, reformist demands (e.g. housing, community action, wages). If the revolutionary party does not engage in such struggles, which are of immediate relevance to ordinary people, it will be cut off from the people it is trying to mobilise. Moreover, people will not become revolutionary in a crisis unless they have experience of struggle. Thus in many of their activities revolutionary parties may not seem very different from other radical groups: it is their political perspective that is different.

Revolution and democracy:[24] The Bolshevik model evidently has very little appeal for the working class in Britain today. None of the parties that follow it has more than a few thousand members; most have only a few hundred. The model suffers because of its association with brutal Stalinist repression. Because of the history of the USSR, left parties find it very difficult to persuade people that a revolution doesn't *necessarily* lead to the loss of liberty. Moreover, 'vanguardism' alienates people because of its elitist, authoritarian connotations.

Recognising this lack of appeal, other socialists (including the Communist Party and some in the Labour left) have reformulated revolutionary strategy away from the Bolshevik 'frontal assault' model. They have swung back towards a more (though not completely) Parliamentary road to socialism. The example of Russia in 1917 is not considered to be very relevant to our present situation. The important difference between Britain (and other advanced capitalist countries) in the seventies and Tsarist Russia is that Britain is a *democracy*, Russia wasn't. Although capitalist democracy does not free the working class from exploitation, the political rights and freedoms it does give are, rightly, very highly prized. Thus socialists cannot hope to gain much support unless they can convince people that socialism means *more*, not less, democracy than capitalism. And to persuade people of this, socialists cannot afford to treat the institutions of capitalist democracy with contempt.

Electing a socialist majority to Parliament is thus seen as highly relevant to the cause of revolution, though not sufficient in itself. In Britain in the foreseeable future, this could only come about through the Labour Party with support from the trade union movement. The strategy, therefore, involves working either inside or outside the Labour Party in order to move it significantly to the left. Even though it remained reformist, a *left-wing* Labour government could bring in changes which shake the system rather than (as in the case of the 1945 government's reforms) strengthen it. For example, an extension of public ownership, *combined with* a real move towards worker democracy, could increase the power and political consciousness of the working class. And this could pave the way for the labour movement to shift further to the left.

Of course, the strategy recognises that the ruling class (with the help, possibly, of foreign governments) would fight back against any government that seriously proposed social and economic change. A revolutionary, rather than left-wing reformist, government would have to tackle the power of the state. Such a government would have to replace the state elites, particularly the military, with its own supporters. It would have to encourage the growth of new institutions — works committees, community councils — parallel to

OUTSIDE... OR ... INSIDE?

existing state institutions, through which its supporters could be mobilised against the inevitable reaction from the privileged classes. The more effective is such a mobilisation, and therefore the more visible is popular support, the less likely are the privileged classes to adopt violence against a democratically elected revolutionary government.

Of course, as far as Britain is concerned, these problems are far in the future. There's no immediate prospect of even a left-wing reformist government being elected, still less a revolutionary one. Nevertheless, a decision to adopt this strategy rather than the Bolshevik model has implications for the type of political action you get involved in now. It means, for example, that action within the Labour Party — trying to move it to the left — is considered to be important, whereas many of the vanguard parties have written off the Labour Party as incapable of being radicalised.

Notes and References

1. S. Prais, *The Evolution of Giant Firms,* (Oxford Economic Papers, 1974).
2. *Royal Commission on the Distribution of Income and Wealth*, Report No. 1., 1975.
3. R. Miliband, *The State in Capitalist Society,* (Quartet, 1969), p. 164.
4. See S. Beharrell and G. Philo, *Trade Unions and the Media,* (Macmillan, 1977).
5. For example, an internal BBC circular of June 1971 refers to Lord Reith's refusal in 1926 to broadcast *anything* which 'might have pro- longed or sought to justify' the General Strike while allowing, 'authentic impartial news of the situation'. This is said to illustrate a principle still relevant to the production of news and current affairs today. See J. Westergaard and M. Riesler, *Class in a Capitalist Society*, (Penguin, 1975), p. 270.
6. Miliband, *op.cit.*
7. 'Uhuru — A Working Alternative,' Uhuru, 1976.
8. See chapter on 'The State and Labour Relations' in Westergaard and Riesler, *op.cit.*
9. See for example the description of attempts by workers at Ford's Halewood plant to achieve job control in H. Beynon, *Working for Ford*, (Penguin, 1973).
10. *Lucas, an alternative Plan,* (IWC Pamphlet No. 54).
11. Mike Cooley, 'Lucas — Socially useful prototypes', *Undercurrents,* 26, Feb—Mar 1978.
12. Information from SERA (Socialist Environment and Resources Associa- tion).
13. See list of groups at the end of this book.
14. See M. Smith, *The Underground in Education,* (Methuen, 1972). Also see list of journals and organisations at the end of this book.
15. See B. Coard, *How the West Indian child is made educationally sub- normal in the British Educational system*, (Caribbean Education & Community Workers Association, 1971).
16. P. Goodman, *Compulsory Miseducation*, (Penguin). See also I. Illich, *Deschooling Society*, (Penguin), and John Holt's books: *How Children Fail* and *Freedom and Beyond*, (both Penguin).
17. In May 1978, Wandsworth Council became Conservative controlled after 7 years of Labour rule. The new Council's policy of selling Council houses has drastically reduced high rise tenants' chances of moving into a house or other low-rise accommodation.
18. See N. Wates, *The Battle for Tolmers Square*, (Routledge and Kegan Paul, 1976).
19. See Jan O'Malley, *The Politics of Community Action*, (Spokesman, 1977). See also C. Cockburn, *The Local State*, (Pluto) and P. Hain, *Radical Regeneration*, (Quartet).
20. See T. Nairn, 'Anatomy of the Labour Party,' in R. Blackburn (ed.) *Revolution and Class Struggle*, (Fontana).
21. See R. Miliband, *op.cit.*
22. See Westergaard and Riesler, *op.cit.*, pp. 252—8. Also Miliband, *op.cit.*
23. See *Labour Research*, January 1979.

24. For further reading on this section, see articles on 'The Future of the Left' in *Socialist Register*, 1977, (Merlin Press). See also *The British Road to Socialism*, (Communist Party of Great Britain); 'Socialists and the Labour Party' by K. Coates, *Socialist Register*, 1973, (Merlin Press); E. Mandel, *From Stalinism to Eurocommunism*, (New Left Books, 1978).

5. What Some People Are Doing

Thinking and acting politically continually involves making personal choices, as I hope the discussion above has shown. Should I work inside or outside the system? Should I concentrate on working for attainable but limited goals, or work for revolutionary change? Can existing well-established groups — political parties and unions — become a radical force, or should I join those who are attempting to create new groups? Is it more important to devote my energies to Third World problems, or should I turn to domestic British issues? Where can I be most effective?

In this chapter, some individuals speak for themselves about what they are doing. Answers to the questions above are implicit in what they say. They have chosen particular activities to get involved in; but, of course, these choices are not immutable. Any politically active person is bound continually to re-evaluate her or his activities, just because there is no certainty about what is the best thing an individual can do. Moreover, the situation is always changing, both because of events in the world outside, and because of developments inside the individual.

The people speaking here haven't been given space because they're 'special' in some way, nor are they being held up as models to be followed. They're ordinary people I just happened to know (or know of) and asked to write something about their activities. After the more abstract argument in the rest of the book, I thought it would be relevant to bring it down to a personal level, and show what particular individuals with a radical political philosophy are *doing* to try to achieve change.

From Cathy:

I spent two years, from 1972 to 1974, working in Vietnam as part of a Quaker team running pre-school playgroups in orphanages. I was a history teacher before that, with little or no experience of pre-school children, and I went to Vietnam with a vague idealistic notion of 'doing something to help the children'. After about a month in Saigon I had lost most of my naivety and realised how much I had to learn from the Vietnamese; after a year I became a cynic and realised how much damage we foreigners were doing;

after two years the Vietnamese people restored some of my idealism and I was ready to come home.

The main messages which I had learned were, firstly that I should tackle some of the problems in my own country, and secondly that the individual does have the power to change society.

I had been warned about the difficulties of coming home, but I was so delighted to be back in Scotland that I was confident that there would be no 'culture shock'. I confess, however, that it was much harder than I had anticipated. There seemed to be a wide gap in understanding between my family and my friends and myself, and it came as a shock to realise that they would *never* fully understand my new attitudes. In a host of subtle and unexpected ways the material values of the West were forced upon me — I still have difficulty watching the 'Generation Game'! And hardest of all to retain through long weeks of unemployment was my belief in the power of the individual to change his own environment.

I was quite determined about two things, however. Firstly, that I would live in Scotland (of which more later), and secondly that I would live in the country. Both of which I am now doing. The de-urbanisation of society; the whole concept embodied in 'Small is Beautiful' had become very important to me.

Now, after three years, I am able to look back and see how I have managed to apply some of what I learned in Vietnam to my own situation at three different levels. Obviously my interest in the international issues of peace and justice remains. I am currently writing a book about foreign aid in Vietnam, and also doing some research for Oxfam into possible aid programmes. Thus the old links are maintained. While in Vietnam, I was horrified by the torture and repression carried out by the old Saigon regime and this has led me to a deep involvement with Amnesty International. In Dumfries we have started up a strong Amnesty Group, and we are also starting a special Campaign Against Torture Group. The Campaign Against the Arms Trade and the anti-nuclear lobby also take up quite a share of my time.

To some it would seem a contradiction for an internationalist to be a Scottish Nationalist, but to me the two are entirely complementary. I believe that Scotland is the right size — in Schumacher terms — and that as a self-determining nation we have a valuable contribution to make to the community of nations. As a virtual colony of England, such development cannot be fully realised. Vietnamese people love their country in a generous outgoing way, and this is why I work for Scottish independence.

Finally, at a local level in Dumfries, I am running a small community information and action centre. This helps to co-ordinate voluntary activity within the community; but, more important, it brings groups together in an effort to promote thinking, action and involvement. Dumfries is a small rural town with typically conservative attitudes. So there is still a long way to go. But all revolutions must start small, and the first step is the important one.

From Ann:

Like so many volunteers, I went overseas straight from University to teach English in a secondary school. My experience in Nigeria was frustrated by competition for examination passes and the conflicting demands of a syllabus, imposing Western culture, hardly relevant even to the elite whom I was teaching. On returning to the UK my first consideration was to re-train in a field more relevant to development and return to a developing country. Moreover, lumbered with a Classics degree, I knew I didn't want to teach the subject in this country – teaching only the academically bright a subject that offers little scope for promoting social change and of no immediate relevance to anybody.

After further consideration, I decided not to look overseas. There is 'under-development' in Britain and after a few weeks back in this country, this became more and more apparent. Having just about rejected the idea of further studies even, and having done a short English as a Foreign Language course, the Returned Volunteer Action Clearing House came up with a job teaching English to Latin American refugees for the Joint Working Group for Refugees from Chile. The organisation operates as a collective whose main concern is reorientation and rehabilitation of political refugees from Latin America. It works in close collaboration with such groups as the Chile Solidarity Campaign, World University Service, Christian Aid and the various Latin American Human Rights Organisations. I took the job.

A knowledge of English gives the refugees the possibility of working, of integrating and contributing to life here, of informing English people about the repressive regimes in Latin America, of discussing their problems with other racial minorities, particularly with other left-wing political refugees – identifying a common struggle, but above all feeling part of a multi-racial Britain.

The Latin America Centre (where I work) holds social and cultural events and acts as an information and advice centre. We see the English classes as exerting a cohesive force, bringing the refugees together to learn the language. This is particularly valuable for those refugees who are not involved in direct political activity, and for the women who might otherwise be at home with the children all day. Creche facilities are available and the centre is frequently visited by Joint Working Group social workers.

To me the teaching is an expression of solidarity. Besides helping the refugees cope with practical matters, it is vital that there is opportunity to discuss the political situation in Latin America in the classroom, so that they gain the confidence to talk about their struggle with English people and other minority groups in this country outside the classroom. The importance of international pressure, adoption of political prisoners, boycotts, campaigns against the arms trade etc. cannot be over-emphasised. It is much more effective for Latin Americans who have experienced the horrors of fascism to speak for themselves when trying to win support here for their struggle. But it is important that they are not always speaking to the converted. Apart from political work through such organisations as the Chile Solidarity Campaign, Amnesty International, trade unions etc it is necessary to establish links with other groups, political and non-political, at a local level, and of course to make contact with individuals.

English people are not very aware of Latin American problems, and it is not very easy for the refugees to break through the traditional English reserve. I see helping the Latin Americans to establish contacts here as an extension of the teaching and as an integral part of broadening the front against fascism and imperialism. Thus my work at the moment is closely related to my volunteer experience with the difference that, as a volunteer, I was supporting the capitalist mode of development, educating the minority of Nigerians who were to have the economic power to wield the political power.

With fascist influences in Britain, with the threat that immigration will be used as a vote-winning issue in the next election, it is important that the refugees' presence in this country be viewed within the context of minority groups in Britain as a whole. No member of any minority group should be prevented from speaking out by not knowing the language or where to get support. Linked to this is the further job of putting pressure on the government to provide adequate facilities for the learning of English and to provide sufficient funds for the refugee programme in general.

From Jo and Peter:

Since working as volunteers in a grassroots community development project in Nicaragua, from 1973 to 1976, we have maintained our interest in Third World and development issues, and attempted to find ways of continuing to contribute to work in these areas.

Shortly after our return from Nicaragua we tried to do some development education work and, during this period, we gave some slide-talks to various groups of people. However, we found this a frustrating and largely ineffectual experience as we were working 'in a vacuum'. We felt there was a need for some kind of follow-up with the groups we made contact with. To be able to do this, we really needed the backing of a larger organisation, whose resources we could call on.

Then, in June 1977, we were invited to a meeting of RVA's Volunteer Programme Working Party (VPWP). We found that we sympathised with RVA's aims and have since become active members, and particularly of the VPWP. We feel that the work of this group is important, as returned volunteers are in a particularly good position to help monitor and evaluate the work of the volunteer-sending agencies.

We have also become actively involved with the University's Third World Society. One of the main roles of the Society is to provide a forum for discussion and investigation of Third World issues among those who are already concerned and interested – many members come from Third World countries. Its other main role is to bring such issues to the attention of other members of the University, to counteract scanty or strongly biased coverage by the mass media.

This year the Society has made quite an impact in the University, especially by means of special events and exhibitions. For instance, at the end of the autumn term, the Society ran a 'Chile Week', with films, and an exhibition in the library foyer, culminating in an evening of Chilean music provided by the group 'Venceremos', which is made up of Chilean exiles. We also rallied some support for the campaign against the arms sale to El Salvador, through the Third World Society: an exhibition was mounted, leaflets were distributed and people were asked to sign petitions, which were later sent to the Ministry of Defence and the Foreign Office. This campaign was an invaluable chance for people to play an active role, and was particularly worthwhile because it was successful — a fact which, hopefully, provided food for thought for the sceptical and the apathetic on the campus, who could not have failed to notice what was going on.

One result of our experience in Nicaragua has been to make us more aware that the Third World is not the only place where 'development' is needed. Many of the problems or, at least, their manifest symptoms, are different here, and for a variety of reasons one feels more powerless to effect change — but the problems are nevertheless just as real.

Since last September, I have been working with a voluntary group which undertakes casework with families experiencing various sorts of difficulty. A wide range of problems are covered: many, though not all, of the cases involve single-parent families, and the nature of the problems may be financial, marital, emotional etc. One case that I am working on involves a 35-year old widow who suffers from agoraphobia (although this is only the central one amongst a host of interrelated problems).

Accordingly, the role played by the volunteer varies in each case — it may be counselling, or take a more practical form such as helping to work out the family budget, or merely be a case of befriending and being a good listener. Liaison with other voluntary and statutory bodies, and putting people in touch with other sources is also important. Whilst I am aware that, at present, we do not always find the best solution to problems, and that there is often a tendency to follow a more 'curative' rather than a 'preventive' line, I feel that the group is becoming more self-critical and that, as time goes on, we shall find more effective ways of working.

We regard these three areas of activity — RVA, the Third World Society and the voluntary casework — as a sort of continuation of the work we were engaged on in Nicaragua. The main difference is that, whereas there we were working full-time in an area of development, now we have other commitments. This can often be frustrating, as on occasion events clash and, generally speaking, we feel we would like to have more time for the activities described above. However, to discontinue our involvement in these areas would be to devalue entirely our 2½ years spent in Nicaragua. 'Volunteering' does not end with stepping off the plane at Heathrow . . .

From Chris:

To start with, I think the world is organised in a fundamentally unjust way, and can only be significantly improved by some kind of revolution. I think, having come to this conclusion, I should do something about it. What can a well educated white middle-class woman do? What should the balance be between 'living my life', i.e. enjoying myself, and 'doing political work'? How far is it necessary to form a grand theory of world revolutionary tendencies (or lack of them) and fit my small town/office/social life into it? How much should I be willing to put myself personally at risk, i.e. of losing friends through boring them, of not eating or sleeping enough, of being arrested — or of being physically hurt? What struggles should I take part in?

I think people have to keep asking these sorts of questions, and talking to other people about them. Otherwise you can become apathetic or lazy, or you can become a maniac political militant isolated from any real contact with other people. (I am the first type of person.)

My answers to these questions, and therefore what I do politically, are based on three things. I believe that politics and personal life are inseparable. I believe we should have some fairly detailed idea of what sort of society we want to achieve 'after a revolution' and struggle to live as much like that as possible. I belong to an oppressed group: women. So I belong to a local support group of Women's Aid, the battered women's organisation. In this organisation I am better at arguing in meetings about the need for all women to gain in self-confidence and self-respect than I am at spending time with individual battered women supporting them and learning from their lives — because I am relatively articulate, used to arguing in front of other people, and because I feel that my happy and comfortable life is light years away from real oppression. A lot of women in Women's Aid feel like this, and it often flares up into a 'class struggle' between the battered women and the rest in which they sometimes feel they are having politics and feminism thrust upon them. These arguments can be exhilarating, in which everyone feels they are understanding each other better, or lacerating.

Besides this kind of argument, in Women's Aid (WA) we have to make practical decisions about our relationship to the State, namely the local authorities and the DHSS. I believe that WA is providing a service which ought to be paid for by the State, so I think it is necessary to demand and, if necessary, force local authorities or the DHSS to pay up. This may mean doing direct action, like squatting in empty council houses to force them to provide a refuge. We also need to work for changes in the laws relating to violence on women: sometimes the only way to do this is again some kind of direct action. This can be frightening — but so is being battered or raped.

I am trying with other friends and my husband to live in a collective non-nuclear family way, to live more cheaply, and to behave to other people less superficially and more generously. I try and get up the courage to talk about these things — and more obviously political things — at work (in the civil service, theoretically a very apolitical place, but in fact laden with assumptions supporting established power structures and life styles).

Why haven't I given up my cushy well-paid job to be a full-time activist (e.g. in Women's Aid, or in an anti-fascist group), or to do some less politically compromising and less alienating job? Many reasons. It's a relatively pleasant way of earning a lot of money, as jobs go. The particular work I do (in planning) is susceptible to small but, I hope, significant amounts of influence towards a more left-wing analysis of urban problems and local and central government's approach to them. I haven't the courage to suddenly try to live on much less money — and I'm not convinced that being poor necessarily leads to being a good revolutionary.

Why don't I join a political party or a revolutionary group? Because I don't really believe that trying to drag the Labour Party to the left will work, and I don't like the politics or style of any of the existing left groups. I don't think that any parties in Britain currently do enough towards enabling people individually and collectively to take power over their own lives, and I think they conversely spend too much time thinking about the theory of what to do nationally.

What has all this got to do with the Third World? *I hope* that, if a 'power to the people' revolution took place in Britain, it would make a difference to the distribution of world power and wealth.

From Sarah:

I was a volunteer in Tanzania for two years — 1972–74. The time spent there has, I feel, changed my whole outlook on England, on education, on individual life style. I returned to England determined to '*do*' things. But the first year was hell: one didn't belong, everything was so large, how was one to act at all?

Now, after well over three years back here, I feel I've achieved the first step — I'm a part of a community. Action perhaps now will not be the imposition of an outsider but something from within. I've taught in the same school for three years. As I do drama at school, I've been able to work in a less formal atmosphere and have been part of a team of people, kids and staff who've staged musicals, working all the time together. A small group, again of staff and kids, have started an Amnesty group, making the school once more a place of questioning.

Out of school I joined my local World Development Movement group. I was at first depressed at how little I could do there. They seemed much older overall, with some having been working for years! Campaigns came and went and one got involved. A returned volunteer has a particular role to play, even if at first it's offering an analysis of this country possible only after removing oneself for a while.

I've also recently become involved with a Christian anti-racist group which has enabled me to enter into what I hope will be an ongoing dialogue.

6. Resources

For those who would like to follow up some of the issues raised in this book in more detail, Rachel Heatley (the author) and RVA have prepared a resources section which is designed to supplement the notes and references in each chapter. This section contains further suggestions for reading, sources of data, practical help and other information, plus addresses of groups concerned with some of the issues mentioned in the text. It is by no means comprehensive, but we hope that it may provide you with a starting point.

Returned Volunteer Action

RVA have also prepared a more comprehensive sheet of suggestions for further study for individuals and groups, with suggestions for related activity. RVA has its own groups around the country plus contacts in most countries where there are British volunteers. Based on the first-hand experience of members, it aims to increase understanding of the causes of inequality and poverty, amongst the British public, by providing speakers, producing education material and organising seminars and conferences, both local and national. It has a resources library and information service providing background material on the kinds of issues discussed in this book, and monitoring and abstracting development magazines and over 200 other periodicals regularly received in the library.

RVA campaigns to change the volunteer and aid programmes in the interests of the poorest, most powerless sectors of Third World countries, and has several working parties on specific parts of those programmes. Where necessary, it undertakes its own evaluation of aid projects in Third World countries.

For full details of its activities, or for the study plan based on this book, contact RVA at:

> Returned Volunteer Action
> 1c Cambridge Terrace
> London NW1 4JL

Some Key Groups to Contact

Anti-Apartheid Movement (AAM)	89 Charlotte Street, London W1P 2DQ.
British Campaign for an Independent East Timor	40 Concannon Road, London SW2.
British Society for Social Responsibility in Science (BSSRS)	9 Poland Street, London W1V 3DG.
Campaign against the Arms Trade (CAAT)	5 Caledonian Road, London N1 9 DX.
Campaign against Poverty and the Arms Trade (COPAT)	c/o CAAT.
Central America Human Rights Committee	59a Church Street, Old Isleworth, Middx.
Counter Information Services (CIS)	9 Poland Street, London W1V 3DG.
Campaign on Basic Human and Democratic Rights in the ASEAN Alliance Countries (COBRA)	6 Endleigh Street, London WC1.
Institute for Workers Control	Bertrand Russell House, Gamble Street, Nottingham NG7 4ET.
Middle East Research and Action Group	5 Caledonian Road, London N1 9DX.
Mozambique, Angola, Guinea Information Centre	34 Percy Street, London W1.
Namibia Support Committee	188 North Gower Street, London NW1.
Returned Volunteer Action (RVA)	1c Cambridge Terrace, London NW1 4JL.
Socialist Environment Resources Association (SERA)	9 Poland Street, London W1V 3DG.
Social Audit	9 Poland Street, London W1V 3DG.
Transnationals Institute	20 Paulus Potterstraat, Amsterdam 1007.
War on Want (WOW)	467 Caledonian Road, London N7 9BG.

Sources of Information

This list is organised broadly according to some of the main themes in the text, although there is inevitably some overlap. Section A under each topic refers to reading matter, and Section B to groups active in that area. Where a book/pamphlet is published by a small group their address is included.

(m)   Magazine or journal
*   For address and full name, see 'Key Groups to Contact' list.

Selling the West to the Third World
A.   Charles Medawar, *Insult or Injury*, (Social Audit, 1979).
      Susan George, *How the Other Half Dies*, (Penguin, 1976).
B.   Social Audit* especially for reports on advertising standards and
          practices.

Physical Control and Repression
A.   Committee on Poverty and the Arms Trade, *Bombs for Breakfast*,
          (COPAT)*, 1978.
      Malcolm Caldwell (ed.), *Ten Years of Military Terror in Indonesia*,
          (Spokesman, 1975).
      Roger Plant, *Guatemala: Unnatural Disaster*, (Latin American Bureau,
          1978).
B.   Campaign against the Arms Trade (CAAT)*
      Amnesty International, 10 Southampton Street, London WC2.
      International Labour Organisation (ILO), 87 New Bond Street,
          London W1.
      Conference on Basic Human and Democratic Rights in the ASEAN
          Alliance Countries (COBRA)*, (for Hong Kong/Thailand/Indonesia/
          East Timor/West Papua/New Guinea/Malaysia/Singapore).
      For Latin America see RVA list.

The Development of Underdevelopment: Colonialism and Neocolonialism
Although there is a very wide literature on this subject most of it is academic
and heavy-going. However, the following are recommended:
A.   A. Gunder Frank, *Lumpen bourgeoisie, lumpen development*, (Monthly
          Review Press).
      W. Rodney, *How Europe Underdeveloped Africa*, (Bogle l'Ouverture,
          1973).
      H. Radice, *International Firms and Modern Imperialism,* (Penguin).
      P. Baran, *The Political Economy of Growth,* (Penguin).
      C. Leys, *Underdevelopment in Kenya,* (Heinemann, 1975). There is a
          summary of the theoretical debate in the first chapter.
      F. Fanon, *The Wretched of the Earth,* (Penguin, 1977).
      Liberation (m), 313/5 Caledonian Road, London N1.
      Race and Class (m), Institute of Race Relations, 247/9 Pentonville
          Road, London N1.

UK Government's Role

A.   Fred Halliday *Iran*, (Penguin, 1978).
      Margolis Rosenhead Shallice and Ackroyd *Technology of Political Control*, (Penguin, 1977).
      R. Barnet, *Intervention and Revolution*, (Paladin, 1972).
      CIS*, *Buying Time in South Africa*.
      International Marxist Group, *Southern Africa in Crisis*, from 328 Upper Street, London N1.
      Red Weekly, *How Labour supports Apartheid*, from 328 Upper Street, London N1.
      Anti-Apartheid Movement*, *Anti Apartheid News*.
      Zimbabwe Information Group, *ZIG Bulletin*, 1 Cambridge Terrace, London NW1.

International Capitalism: Multinationals in the Third World
Again there is an enormous volume of literature on the subject. Some of the main sources of information are:—
B.   War on Want*, for reports on the drug companies, baby foods, tobacco, tea.
      Counter Information Services*, especially the report on ITT's attempt to subvert Allende's Government in Chile and Anti-reports on many multinationals.
      Social Audit*, On the Avon Rubber Co. Ltd., 1976.
      Transnationals Information Exchange, c/o War on Want.
More detailed information can be obtained from groups or sources concerned with specific geographical areas.

Modernisation without Social Revolution
A.   Haslemere Group, *Death of the Green Revolution*, c/o War on Want.
      Federation of UK and Eire Malaysian and Singapore Students Organisation (FUEMSSO), *Singapore: behind the economic miracle*, c/o COBRA.*
      M. Caldwell and M. Austin, *Malaysia: the making of a neo-colony*, (Spokesman, 1977).

Socialism and Repression
A.   Joseph Hanson, *Dynamics of the Cuban Revolution*, (Pathfinder, 1978).
      S. Schram, *Mao Tse-Tung*, (Penguin, 1966).
      J. Myrdal, *Report from a Chinese Village*, (Pan, 1975).

Aid
A.   S. Weissman, *The Trojan Horse*, (Pacific Studies Centre and Northern American Congress on Latin America, Ramparts, 1975).
      Latin America Bureau, *Britain and Latin America*, 1979.
      Glyn Roberts, *Questioning Development*, (from RVA).

Cheryl Payer, *The Debt Trap*, (Penguin, 1974).
T. Hayter, *Aid as Imperialism*, (Penguin, 1974) (now out of print but
    may be available in libraries).
B.   Returned Volunteer Action*

Repression in the UK
A.   Margolis, Rosenhead, Ackroyd and Shallice, *The Technology of Political
        Control*, (Penguin, 1977).
    Rights (m), National Council for Civil Liberties, 186 Kings Cross Road,
        London WC1X 9DE.
    State Research Bulletin (m), State Research, 9 Poland Street,
        London W1V 3DG.

Action in the UK: Alternatives
A.   *Ways and Means* (directory), Student Community Action, National
        Union of Students (SCANUS), 1978.
    In the making (directory of new projects), 84 Church Street, Wolverton,
        Milton Keynes.
    Undercurrents (m), 27 Clerkenwell Close, London EC1R 0AT.
    Whole Earth (m), 11 George Street, Brighton BN2 1RH.
B.   Future Studies Centre, 15 Kelso Road, Leeds LS2 9PC.
    Industrial Common Ownership Movement, 31 Hare Street, London SE18.
    Institute for Workers Control*
    Centre for Alternative Industrial and Technological Systems, North
        East London Polytechnic, Longbridge Road, Dagenham.
    Socialist Environment Resources Association.*

Action in the UK: Radical Professions
(i) Education
A.   Mike Smith, *The Underground in Education*, (Methuen, 1977).
    Radical Education (m), 86 Eleanor Road, London E8.
    Teaching London Kids (m), 40 Hamilton Road, London SW19.
    Rank and File Teacher (m), 5 Rommany Road, London SW27.

(ii) Health and Social Development
A.   *Medicine in Society* (m), 16 King Street, London WC2.
B.   Association of Radical Midwives, 17 Fairfax Road, Derby.
    Socialist Medical Association, 9 Poland Street, London W1V 3DG.
    Radical Statistics Group, c/o BSSRS*.
    See also comprehensive list covering alternative groups and journals
        on community and women's health care, and patients participation,
        available from RVA.

(iii) Technology/Science
See also under Alternatives.
A.   *Science for people* (m), BSSRS*.
B.   British Society for Social Responsibility in Science (BSSRS)*.

(iv) Agriculture
B.   Agricapital Group, c/o BSSRS*.

(v) Trade Unions
A.   *Where were you brother?* (War on Want*, 1978).
          Workers Control (m), Institute for Workers Control*.
B.   Trade Union International Research Group, Ruskin Hall, Dunstan Road, Old Headington, Oxford OX3 9BZ.

(vi) Community Action
A.   *Community Action* (m), P O Box 665, London SW1X 81Z.
          Community Development Programme Pamphlets on different areas of the country available from socialist bookshops (the CDP has now been closed down) or from the Home Office, 50 Queen Anne's Gate, (Room 1373), London SW1.
B.   Groups are generally very localised. See *Ways and Means*, SCANUS, for more details, or look in your local socialist bookshop.

Some Useful Tools
For further suggestions, see RVA's leaflet.
S. Alinsky, *Rules for Radicals*, (Vintage, 1973).
P. Hain, *Radical Regeneration*, (Quartet, 1975), Chapter 8 on Radical Tactics.
Community Action, *Investigators Handbook*, and supplements, *Community Action*, P O Box 665, London SW1X 8DZ.
People's News Service, Oxford House, Derbyshire St., London E2.

Sources of Data and Specialised Libraries
Ruth Leger Sivard, *World Military and Social Expenditure*, (annual edition) (available from CAAT*).
Organisation for Economic Co-operation in Development, *Geographical Distribution of Financial Flows to Developing Countries* (OECD, Paris).
Food and Agricultural Organisation, *Trade Yearbook* and *Production Yearbook* FAO, Via del Terme di Caracalla, Rome 00100.
Inequality in Britain Today and *Labour Research* (monthly), Labour Research Department, LRD 78 Blackfriars Road, London SE1 8H7.
Royal Commission on the distribution of Income and Wealth, H.M.S.O.
Contemporary Archive on Latin America, 1 Cambridge Terrace, London NW1.
Institute of Race Relations, 247–9 Pentonville Road, London N1.